ML Answers the 101 Most-Asked Questions

The Liturgical Music Answer Book

Peggy Lovrien

D1417353

Resource Publications, Inc.
San Jose, California

© 1999 Resource Publications, Inc. All rights reserved. No part of this book may be photocopied or otherwise reproduced without permission from the publisher. For reprint permission, contact:

Reprint Department
Resource Publications, Inc.
160 E. Virginia Street #290
San Jose, California 95112-5876
(408) 286-8505 voice
(408) 287-8748 fax

Library of Congress Cataloging-in-Publication Data
Lovrien, Peggy, 1952–
    The liturgical music answer book / Peggy Lovrien.
      p.   cm. — (ML answers the 101 most-asked questions)
    Includes bibliographical references and index.
    ISBN 0-89390-454-6 (pbk.)
    1. Church music—Catholic Church—Instruction and study.
    2. Catholic Church—Liturgy—Study and teaching.   I. Title.
    II. Series.
    MT88.L695   1999
    264'.0202—dc21   99-27873
                                                CIP

Printed in the United States of America

99 00 01 02 03 | 5 4 3 2 1

Editorial director: Nick Wagner
Prepress manager: Elizabeth J. Asborno
Production coordinator: Mike Sagara

Excerpts from the English Translation of *The Lectionary for Mass* © 1969, 1981, International Committee on English in the Liturgy, Inc. (ICEL); excerpts from the English Translation of *The Roman Missal* © 1973, ICEL. All rights reserved.

Excerpts from *Environment and Art in Catholic Worship* Copyright © 1978 United States Catholic Conference, Inc. (USCC), Washington, DC; *Music in Catholic Worship* © 1983 USCC; and *Liturgical Music Today* © 1982. All rights reserved.

Excerpts from *Visions of Liturgy and Music for a New Century* and *Liturgical Inculturation: Sacramentals, Religiosity, and Catechesis* Copyright © 1996 by The Order of St. Benedict, Inc. Published by The Liturgical Press, Collegeville, Minnesota. Used with permission.

"When I call to mind the tears I shed
at the songs of Thy Church
at the outset of my recovered faith,
and how even now I am moved not by the singing
but by what is sung,
when they are sung
with a clear and skillfully modulated voice,
I then acknowledge the great utility of this custom....
...I feel that our souls are moved
to the ardor of piety
by the sacred words
more piously and powerfully
when these words are sung
than when they are not sung."

St. Augustine
Confessions, Book X, Chapter 33

Contents

Implementing Liturgical Music

Questions from Choir Leaders and Members

Questions from Pastors and Pastoral Leaders

Paying Liturgical Music Directors

Questions from the Assembly

Many Cultures, One Mass

Groundwork Questions

1. What is liturgical music?

The Catholic liturgy is musical. Singing the liturgy and making music is the work of the people. The people sing the texts of the word of God and the texts and rites of the liturgy. The assembly of believers has a central role in singing the liturgy. In the liturgy believers join the texts of the liturgy to the rite to express faith.

The most important goal for music leaders is to enable the assembled to participate in the liturgy in a full, active, and conscious manner. At Sunday Mass, a wedding, a funeral, a celebration of confirmation or baptism, the people must sing the liturgy. Singing the liturgy and its rites is a normal dimension of every experience of communal worship. It is very important that the people sing because the action of singing the liturgy forms Christians. When they sing the liturgy, they express and deepen their faith.

Liturgical music enhances the texts and rituals of the liturgy and moves the assembly to unity. We abandon individualism to join the community of singing believers. We choose music that enables the community to sing its faith in unity. We re-evaluate the use of any music that falls short of moving the singing assembly to unity and faith.

The term "liturgical music" may have first appeared in the United States in the document *Music in Catholic Worship*, produced by the American Bishops' Committee on the Liturgy.

2. Why did Vatican II emphasize that the people should be singing?

Citing 1 Peter 2:9, the Second Vatican Council asserted that the people should participate in the liturgy fully, consciously, and actively. It asserted that from baptism the Christian has a right and duty to active participation in the liturgy. It instructs church leaders to make active participation in the liturgy the goal before all other goals. When an assembly of believers sings the liturgy, they are actively participating in the liturgy and expressing their faith. Expressing faith deepens faith.

In the years leading up to the Second Vatican Council, the people did not sing or respond during Sunday Mass. The people were passive spectators who watched the priest and servers do the liturgy and perform the dialogue of responses and acclamations. Only the choir sang. The people listened. Only the priests and deacons could proclaim the Scriptures. Catechists instructed Catholics to come to hear the Mass. The people understood that ministry was something reserved for the priests, brothers, and sisters. These practices limited the people's notion of personal responsibility to spread the kingdom of justice in their daily lives.

Upon reflection, our church leaders understood that listening to music and responses is a passive position more suited for the concert hall than for a gathering of believers expressing and deepening their faith as a community.

After the Second Vatican Council, we have found that active participation in a well-planned celebration of the liturgy has the power to form people in the faith and strengthen them to evangelize society in faith. Active participation can convince the people of God that ministry is their business.

The purpose of singing the liturgy is to proclaim the message and to express human feelings. It involves the singer's power of rational thinking and the deepest domain of the heart to create an ambience of beauty.

We sing the rites, we respond, we proclaim the word of God, we process, and we share in the Body and Blood of Christ. The presider dismisses us to continue our ministry (the mission of Christ) into the world as the Body of Christ. We are the ministers responsible for building the kingdom in the world. We go forth to evangelize.

> **3.** *I have heard the terms "sacred music" and "liturgical music." Is there a difference?*

The two terms "sacred music" and "liturgical music" both refer to music in the liturgy. However, the terms indicate a shift in the way the church talked about music in the liturgy before the Second Vatican Council and the way it talks about it after the Second Vatican Council.

During the first three centuries of the church, church leaders taught that music is the servant of religion. Music for the liturgy was called "sacred music." The music was sacred only when it opened the minds of the faithful to Christian teachings and prepared the heart to ponder upon thoughts of the sacred realm. Instrumental music, on the other hand, was outlawed in the church because there was no text to convert the hearts of the faithful.

Once the church settled in Rome during the sixth to the ninth century, the church defined music for the liturgy as sacred (vs. profane music of the public sphere.) With the help of Benedictine research and resources, Pope Gregory I organized the liturgy in the sixth century. He assigned particular chants to the texts of liturgies during the liturgical year. European church composers of the known world wrote simple chant music for the psalms, canticles, and hymn texts of liturgy and Scripture.

Later, Pope Pius X (1903–1914) gathered church officials together, and they outlined the way composers could write music and implement music in the liturgy (see the document *Tra le*

5

Sollecitudini). The composers of sacred music had to be approved by Rome. The composers on this list were also only European. With this kind of control, Rome set up a system of criteria and standards which they believed allowed them to objectively judge the sacred or profane nature of music.

In this century, the Second Vatican Council produced the *Constitution on the Sacred Liturgy* (December 4, 1963), which re-articulated Pope Pius X's value that the people and their active participation in the liturgy is primary in order to instill the true Christian spirit. It says that "to promote active participation, the people should be encouraged to take part by means of acclamations, responses, psalmody, antiphons, and songs, as well as by actions, gestures, and bearing" (CSL 30).

The assembly replaced the choir as the primary singers of the liturgy. As a result, the church's theology expressed in the texts shapes Catholics as they express it in song.

This perspective, and the celebration of the liturgy in the language of the people, expanded our idea about music for the liturgy. Church leaders were convinced that the sung text would activate a deeper conversion in the hearts of all people singing in their own language (instead of the Latin language, which was the only language allowed in the liturgy up until that time). Church leaders believed that this kind of conversion would lead Catholics to acceptance of the mission of Christ. One who accepts the mission of Christ will move into the world to transform the world (building the kingdom of God.) As a result, singing in the vernacular was essential.

The document also embraced music formed by people of the various cultures of the world. Rome would no longer control an approved list of composers of liturgical music. As a result, universal Catholic music became multi-cultural.

Later, in the United States, the American bishops' document *Liturgical Music Today* affirmed the use of the term "liturgical music." This term refers to music as integral to the liturgy. They said that liturgical music connotes action and involvement of people. It helps the people to express and shape their faith through the liturgy. Because Catholics sing the liturgy, we refer to the music as "liturgical music."

The Music Ministry

4. What is the role of the cantor?

The cantor is a facilitator and an instructor. The cantor encourages the singing assembly. This minister has the skills to teach new music to the assembly. The cantor functions when there is no choir to lead the assembly to sing the liturgy. The cantor focuses his or her attention on the people to ensure that they are successfully singing.

Liturgical Music Today also describes a role distinct from that of the cantor. It says that the psalmist would sing the verses of the responsorial and communion psalm. It goes on to say, "Frequently, the two roles will be combined in one person" (LMT 69).

The cantor or psalmist sings the verses of the psalms so that every word is clearly delivered. Like a good presider who enfleshes the text of a prayer with human emotion and expression, the cantor enfleshes the text of a psalm. It is the responsibility of the cantor to use the Bible and other sources to study the historical background of the psalms so that when one is sung, the cantor knows who sang it in biblical times and for what reason. A cantor is well prepared. A cantor is a minister of care who presents a psalm after praying over it for a week, studying its place in the tradition, and considering every nuance of its musical setting. This method takes time and allows the cantor to internalize the psalm. When the psalm is sung, the cantor sings it from his or her heart. This is a ministry, a labor of love, which influences and forms faith.

The cantor must resist the temptation to draw attention to his or her musical abilities. Music in the liturgy is a communal, not individual, work. Instead, these abilities, the result of talent and hard work, are given over to the community and the liturgy as an avenue of approach to the presence of God. Although the community may and should appreciate the cantor's abilities, those abilities are best used to help the assembly to participate actively and to sing with a full voice. The cantor should understand the importance of active participation of the assembly so that the assembly is drawn into the center of worship.

The cantor sets up a sung dialogue between the people and the cantor, or between the people and the priest, and sometimes between the people themselves. The dialogue takes place in song using texts or liturgical chants and acclamations. Musical dialogue is important in the liturgy because dialogue infers relationship and relationship infers the presence of a community.

To enable the song of the assembly, the cantor is an animator who uses gesture to signal the entrance of the singing assembly. His or her face expresses an engaged and enthusiastic participant in the song. If the cantor uses a sound system (which we find in most churches), he or she is careful not to make his or her voice the primary sound in the song of the assembly. The cantor might lead the assembly into the first phrase of a known hymn or refrain but then back away from the microphone so that the organ or piano will accompany the sung voices of the primary choir, the assembly. The cantor's voice should not be amplified all the time. The assembly should hear themselves sing without the cantor's voice dominating the assembly.

Some folks wonder if it is appropriate for the organist or pianist to also be the cantor. An organist or a pianist should lead the music through the instrument only.

The *Constitution on the Sacred Liturgy* makes it clear that "each one, minister or layperson, who has an office to perform, should do all of, but only, those parts which pertain to that office by the nature of the rite and the principles of liturgy" (CSL 28). The priest does not proclaim the first two readings or the psalm and, likewise, the cantor does not play the instrument.

When there is a choir, the choir, as a group, functions much like the cantor.

5. What is the role of the liturgical choir director?

A liturgical choir director knows by experience Catholic prayer (the Mass and sacramental celebrations) and the celebrations of feasts and seasons of the liturgical year. This person should have a deep love for the mission of Jesus, which commits her or him to promoting that mission in every aspect of the person's life and ministry.

The goal of the liturgical musicians is full, conscious, and active participation of every Catholic in the liturgy (*Constitution on the Sacred Liturgy* 14). The document *Liturgical Music Today* states that the "entire worshiping assembly exercises a ministry of music" (63). This is achieved through the dialogue of sung prayer among the people, the presider, and the choir or cantor. The primary choir is the assembly who sings the liturgy. The director is concerned even if there is only one person in the assembly who is not singing.

The director convenes singers of faith (believers) to make up a choir who express their faith as they minister. The director chooses sound, well-formed, liturgical music to enable the choir to express the depth and beauty of its faith. In the meantime, the director does ongoing musical formation and catechetical formation for choir members.

I like to think of the director as a co-presider of the liturgy, a liturgical musician, a teacher of music, a teacher of the liturgy, a vehicle for Catholic formation of the members, and a spiritual guide.

The liturgical choir director is different from a choir director in a school or university because the focus of music-making is unique. A liturgical choir director works with music to help the assembly sing the rite in the liturgy, which lifts up the hearts of believers and moves them to conversion and mission.

6. What is the role of the choir?

A choir is a group of disciples who are musicians. Their goal is to enliven the faith of each person in the assembly by moving each person to sing and express his or her faith.

The choir supports and encourages the song of the assembly.

The choir member is "first a disciple and then a minister. The musician belongs first of all to the assembly; he or she is a worshiper.... He or she is a minister...who shares faith, serves the community, and expresses the love of God and neighbor through music" (LMT 64).

Every member of a liturgical choir should receive training as a cantor. Then, as a member of the choir, every individual is able to animate and encourage the assembly's song through gesture, facial expression, and song. A member of a liturgical choir cannot be expressionless. Every member is responsible for setting up a dialogue in sung prayer with the assembly.

Each member of a choir faithfully participates in weekly rehearsals. He or she arrives early before the liturgy for prayer and vocal warm-up to prepare for the liturgy. Members of the choir should have all their music ready and organized for the liturgy and either listen to or be involved in the prelude music ten to fifteen minutes before the liturgy.

A liturgical choir is more concerned with ways to foster a dialogue of music between itself, the assembly, and the presider in the liturgy. This concern outweighs the desire to perform for the assembly.

The choir works like a group of cantors to introduce new music, to teach the assembly how to participate in the liturgy actively, and to encourage the assembly to sing (see LMT 68).

7. What is the role of the organist?

A good liturgical organist knows the organ very well. The organist knows how to play hymnody well, how to improvise, and how to play the classics. This person is an expert with hymnody, acclamations, song, psalms, choir music and organ music.

An organist knows music theory very well, thus making it possible to be musically flexible. This person is a master in transposition so that accompaniment can be adjusted to a singing range most successful for the assembly. The organist knows the assembly well and is able to identify the registrations and playing styles that encourage and support the assembly as they sing the liturgy. A very good organist is humble about the technique acquired through years of study; it takes maturity to use this well-formed technique to help the assembly sing with ease without pointing to oneself.

Through pastoral ministry, the organist learns how to be flexible with people, managing to teach them about liturgical music and the liturgy with diplomacy.

The organist serves the assembly by prayerfully leading them into an experience of beauty. The goal is to serve the community's prayer.

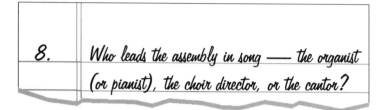

8. *Who leads the assembly in song — the organist (or pianist), the choir director, or the cantor?*

Among these three ministers, the organist leads when the assembly sings the liturgy. An organist for the Catholic tradition is a "liturgical organist" who is well formed in the liturgy.

The best situation exists when a liturgical choir director and the organist are equally equipped to make decisions about music during the liturgy. There can be an ongoing ebb and flow of leadership. When the choir sings the verses of the song during communion, for example, the organist might yield to the choir director's tempo, interpretation, and dynamic. But when the assembly's part comes into play, the choir and director yield to the organist's leadership.

All of this can happen if they plan as a team, rehearse regularly with one another, and focus their ministry on the primary choir, the assembly. Liturgical musicians have to have enough ego to comfortably share an intimate experience of music-making in public and still enough humility to be able to yield to others at the appropriate times.

Basic Instruments
Of the Liturgy

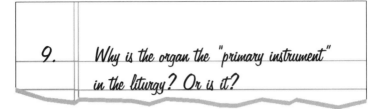

9. Why is the organ the "primary instrument" in the liturgy? Or is it?

The primary instrument in the liturgy is the voice of the assembly (the people, the priest, the choir, the cantor, and all other ministries). The organ can sustain the key, melody, and rhythm of songs or acclamations they sing. It can lead and accompany the assembly as they sing the liturgy.

In the time of the early church, the organ was used in non-church settings. Music in the church was only vocal music. After Pope Gregory VI revised the vocal chants in the sixth century, the church gradually accepted the organ into the liturgy in the eighth and ninth centuries to accompany the chants. The church gradually used the organ and other musical instruments to enhance singers and the beauty of Gregorian chant (*Musicae Sacrae*). Only those instruments approved by Rome could be used in the liturgy. Even though the church gradually accepted the use of the organ, it would not allow various percussion instruments. These instruments were considered by Rome to be secular instruments, not sacred. As the faith spread to other lands, this judgment must have seemed strange to those cultures in which percussion instruments were considered sacred instruments.

The criteria for the use of various instruments in the liturgy changed as history unfolded. The organ, once used in brothels during the days of the early church, later became the only instrument suited for the liturgy. Yet while the sounds of various stops on the organ imitated brass, strings, and woodwinds, those actual instruments were not allowed until a later time in history. After the piano was invented, it too was considered profane and was not allowed in the liturgy for decades.

Due to the universal nature of the church in the world, sensitivity to various cultures in the world shaped a new attitude about instruments for the liturgy. The criteria for liturgical instruments expanded to include those judged suitable by the local bishop

Although the organ is highly regarded, it is no longer considered the only instrument capable of uplifting the hearts of believers or of facilitating participation.

10. *Do we have to use the organ at all?*

If there is no one in the parish who knows how to play the organ, one could research music for manuals only (keyboard without pedals.) It is important to use the organ, but use it tastefully so that the beauty of the instrument is not ignored.

Don't force a piano player to play the organ. One who does not understand and love the instrument can do damage to an assembly's understanding of the sound of an organ. If the instrument is played poorly, then the people's experience of the instrument is negative. If the person is not interested in the instrument, find someone else who is.

11. *Nobody plays organ in our parish. What should we do?*

You can help the future of your parish with some thoughtful and careful planning. The goal, to get people from the parish to play the organ, can happen with a plan.

If you have a pipe organ in your church, find out all you can about its builder and about pipe organs in general.

Next, start asking around to discover the ninth- and tenth-grade students who play the piano. Get to know the student and his or her family.

Locate the nearest American Guild of Organists chapter, call them, and ask for the dates and locations of the next organ concert.

Invite high school students and their families to the concert and make certain that you arrive early enough to get a place in the middle of the room or church so you can get the full advantage of the sound. Then, let the sound convert the young people. (If these students or these families aren't converted, don't give up hope. Seek out others and try again. It will work one day.) When you find a student with an enthusiastic response to the instrument, you are on your way.

Either find a sponsor or be a sponsor to finance organ lessons for the youth (if Mom and Dad can't manage it). Next, talk with the liturgical organists at other Catholic churches or with the AGO members and ask them who their teachers are. You can get good ideas about a teacher for the student.

Call an organ tuner and have your church organ assessed and tuned. Young musicians deserve to practice on a tuned instrument.

Go to your locksmith and make a fancy key to the organ. Present this special key to the young person with a coupon for ten pre-paid organ lessons. The permission and cooperation of the parents, of course, is essential.

If you have the talent yourself, you could also study the instrument at the same time. Be thoughtful about the needs of the church in the future. One who ministers should always teach at least one or more younger persons how to grow into the ministry.

12. Which other instruments are appropriate to facilitate the song of the assembly?

Although the *Constitution on the Sacred Liturgy* says that the organ is to be highly regarded, other instruments can be used in the liturgy. We can use clarinet, flute, oboe, trumpet, tuba, trombone, saxophone, violin, guitar, harp, and percussion instruments, to name a few. Instruments can be used with an organ, piano, or folk ensemble. Instruments, like musicians, should enable the assembly to sing the liturgy. When the liturgy stops or the sung liturgy is interrupted because of the use of an instrument, its use is inappropriate.

An ensemble, for example, can make use of a piano, a flute or two, a trumpet, a bass, a couple of rhythm guitars, violins, and percussion instruments. The leader is the convener of all musicians in the ensemble and monitors the quality of the group's accompaniment for the assembly as well as the quality of relationships among group members. An ensemble like this functions as a unit to accompany and enhance the assembly as they sing the liturgy.

Folk ensembles (or instrumental ensembles) and choirs can use the triangle, the tambourine, a wood block, a gong, glockenspiels, or a tympani.

Various instruments allow a director to paint sound pictures with the music in order to enhance conversion as the assembly sings the liturgy.

13. *Can we use the piano to accompany hymns when we have no organist?*

Yes, you can use the piano to accompany hymns. However, keep in mind that most of the music for hymns was arranged for the organ, so if you are asking a pianist to play, he or she will need a lot of lead time to figure out how to rearrange certain parts in the hymn to handle it on the piano. Some sections are impossible for even the most accomplished pianist to manage, so the pianist needs to rearrange the music in those sections.

14. *What kind of piano should the church have?*

There are many shapes and brands of pianos from which to choose. How to determine which is the best for your parish takes some time and research.

Ask for your church's blueprints to find out how many square feet in your church you need to fill with sound. The size of the church affects the size of piano you need. Make a file and note whether the church is carpeted and whether the chairs are upholstered. These materials soak up sound.

Read about pianos. Go to the library and check out Larry Fine's book, *The Piano Book: Buying and Owning a New or Used Piano*. This book is a consumer's guide to buying a piano.

Talk with a piano teacher or two from the local college music department (if your town doesn't have a college, make an appointment with one from the nearest college). Ask this person which three piano brands he or she likes to play on and why.

Find the two or three liturgical musicians in the area who use piano in the liturgy. Ask them about the kinds and sizes of pianos they've used in churches and which they prefer.

21

It is also a good idea to talk with a piano tuner or two and ask which piano lasts well over time. Let him or her know how often you plan to use the piano and whether the church is evenly heated in the winter (some churches turn off the heat during the week, which is very hard on an instrument in the colder climates.)

After these steps, go and play on the pianos recommended by your research and contacts. Be prepared to play the same song on each piano so you can compare the touch and tone of the instrument. If you did your research, you will shop well prepared.

15. How can I help our committee purchase a new piano?

Whenever a parish committee considers a major purchase such as a piano, members should pray for unity within diverse perspectives, study about pianos until a consensus is formed, raise funds, and then purchase. The prayer should be ongoing: at every meeting, before each visitation and listening session, and before the actual purchase.

Study requires that committee members commit to reading product descriptions and other resources about pianos. A good resource book is *The Piano Book: Buying and Owning a New or Used Piano* by Larry Fine.

Shopping involves going into stores, warehouses, other churches or schools to listen to a particular brand-name piano. Make certain you try various brands, including Steinway. When you know what a Steinway sounds like, you can judge the quality of sound of other instruments.

You will want to schedule visits with the same parish pianist or organist who can inform non-players of her or his judgment of the instrument. It doesn't work to "take turns" with two or more different pianists showing at different times. The player needs to experience all brands of pianos you consider so she or he can judge by comparison. Study also means interviewing one or more piano tuners, asking them which piano they like to work with and why and which stands the test of time, temperature, and use.

Raising funds for the piano should be ongoing, but at this point the committee will know how much money is needed. Choose the piano because of the quality of the instrument and the size needed for the church room. Start with that information and then set the budget—not vice versa.

When the committee has prayed and has studied, the next step is to determine which person on the committee has the talent to make a deal with the seller. One who is good at dealing over the purchase of a car might have the gifts for arranging a deal with the piano salesperson.

Finally, enjoy your new piano now in the service of God and God's people.

| 16. | *Sometimes, the piano arrangement for a song or hymn is too hard. I can make up my own accompaniment to music the assembly sings, can't I?* |

Sometimes pianists make up an accompaniment for a melody line that has only guitar symbols to suggest harmonization. Some pianists do an adequate job while others excel at improvisation. Good improvisation, however, requires substantial knowledge of music theory.

Pianists need to avoid the temptation to improvise on all music or to ignore a written accompaniment. A well-rounded liturgical pianist is capable of sight-reading a written accompaniment, choral setting, hymn, song, or acclamation. Pianists should work out the composer's accompaniment before introducing their own improvised accompaniment. It may be a poor choice to improvise when a good accompaniment already exists.

Improvisation, however, is an important skill for any liturgical organist or pianist. In order to support the singing assembly or to play with folk ensembles, pianists fill in the bass line and harmonization.

Implementing
Liturgical Music

17. How can we get the assembly to sing well?

To get a Catholic assembly to sing well, the people need an established repertoire of liturgical music which they love to sing. These songs need to be repeated throughout the seasons of the liturgical year. A solid and enduring liturgical music repertoire shapes and forms the people who love to sing it in Christian spirituality (the paschal mystery).

To get the assembly to sing well, the parish repertoire of liturgical music people love to sing has to begin with careful planning. (See Question 18 for details.) A music minister should be delegated with the responsibility to choose and shape the assembly's repertoire and organize it so the assembly can sing songs fitting for each season of the liturgical year and for strengthening them on their journey in faith. I believe that the importance of this is under-rated. The parish repertoire of liturgical music shapes Catholic spiritually. If the repertoire is weak or poorly organized, it can spiritually deform the assembly. The assembly needs to be able to sing from a well-organized list built on the liturgical year. It needs to repeat music often to build a repertoire they can know well. Repeating sung texts throughout the liturgical year is the foundation of a strong singing assembly.

The assembly needs a faith-filled, competent musician who understands the rites of the liturgy and chooses appropriate music to express the rites. The musician should be capable of studying, teaching about, and leading liturgical music. A liturgical musician teaches other musicians to draw the assembly into the center of worship to sing the liturgy.

At least some of the assembly need access to both text and music. I recommend the use of a hymnal which can unify the assembly. While the assembly draws its repertoire from a hymnal, the choir draws from many sources for the music they use to embellish the assembly's song. It is always good practice to plan music that the people can learn by rote.

The parish needs a good organ and piano which are well maintained and well placed within the assembly. If the parish uses an ensemble, they deserve musicians who can capably handle the instruments they use (such as guitar, flute, bass, drums, percussion instruments, etc.).

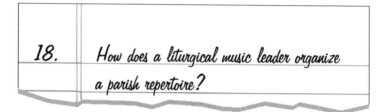

18. *How does a liturgical music leader organize a parish repertoire?*

A liturgical music leader should convene all music leaders in the parish to do planning for the coming liturgical year. Together, they should make a list of hymns, songs, and acclamations the assembly sings well. The goal is to have one repertoire list everyone uses and avoid having a different list for each Mass time. Working together, the leader facilitates the following:

• Outline the whole liturgical year: Advent, Christmas, winter Ordinary Time, Lent, the Triduum, the Easter season (the Sundays of Easter including Pentecost), and summer Ordinary Time.

• Make a list of six seasonal songs for each season that the assembly already knows. (Choose those most recognized by all Mass times.) Include six general gathering hymns or songs people sing almost by heart.

• For the eucharistic prayer acclamations, list at least three settings of the Holy they know, three settings of the memorial acclamation they know, and three settings of the Amen they know. Choose a Holy, memorial acclamation, and Amen that are in the same key and plan to use them together. One can also use one Mass setting written by one composer on the same musical idea.

If you must teach the assembly three complete sets of acclamations, consider teaching one first and using it the whole year. Add a new set the second year and the third year.

After three years you will have three sets of acclamations for the eucharistic prayer that the assembly knows well.

- For acclamations during the communion rite, list three settings of the Lamb of God they already know and six communion psalms or songs people sing almost by heart. List a choice of six well-known hymns the people can stand to sing after the communion procession to give thanks for the Eucharist just celebrated. Hymns are designed in such a way that it is possible to sing one melody and use a variety of texts. As a result, the tune is not limited to one season of the church year. (See Question 19 below regarding the use of hymns with other texts.)

After you outline the above information, you have a picture of a three-year repertoire for the assembly. Allow the assembly to get comfortable with the music over one three-year cycle of readings with just this list.

Next, work with the choir director to list which hymns or songs can be embellished by the choir with four-part harmony or descants. Then, list five or six pieces the choir sings as a group per season for prelude, occasional presentation of gifts, and postlude.

Remember that the goal of a parish choir is to get every person in the assembly to sing with gusto. Choir members may say that they are bored singing the same old music with the assembly. However, a fixed repertoire is an opportunity for the choir or ensemble to have fun learning the vocal parts so the assembly could sing the melody and the choir sing alto, tenor (with sopranos), and bass (sometimes doubled with altos an octave higher).

Thoughtful, patient planning can make singing fun and easy for the assembly.

19. *I've heard there is a way to use hymn tunes with various texts. How do I do that?*

A good hymnal will have a number of indices to assist your planning. One is a metrical index of tunes. It tells us how many syllables there are in each hymn line. Look at your copy of "Joyful, Joyful, We Adore Thee." Below the hymn is fine print indicating who wrote the text. Below that is the name of the tune HYMN TO JOY, followed by 8 7 8 7 D. Now, count the syllables in the first two measures, "Joyful, joyful, we adore thee." There are eight syllables. In the next two measures, "God of glory, Lord of love," we count seven syllables. Every four measures will have the same pattern, eight syllables followed by seven syllables. This is a key for using other texts to this tune. It is called a metrical index because the meter of the poetry follows this pattern.

The metrical index helps the planner to use one melody but many texts. To illustrate this, I will list some possibilities. For example, the planner could have the assembly sing "Joyful, Joyful, We Adore Thee" (hymn tune: HYMN TO JOY) but use the words of the hymn "Love Divine, All Loves Excelling" because both of them have the same metrical setting, 8 7 8 7 D. If the assembly knows few Marian hymns, you can use the same hymn tune, HYMN TO JOY, with the text "Sing of Mary, Pure and Lowly." You can use the same hymn tune with the text, "There's a Wideness in God's Mercy," "Blessed Feasts of Blessed Martyrs," "Lord, Whose Love in Humble Service," "Lord, You Give the Great Commission," and "God, Who Stretched the Spangled Heavens," to name a few. As a result, you can teach the assembly one tune and celebrate different themes, seasons of the year, or rites with other texts. In your hymnal's "Metrical Index of Tunes," you will find these and more interchangeable hymn texts and tunes. Of course, the musician has to discern whether the tune suits the mood of the text and the season.

While the organist or pianist plays a familiar melody of a hymn, the assembly can sing different texts to support the season. As a result, the assembly may know one melody but use many texts to sing about different seasons of the year or different sacramental celebrations.

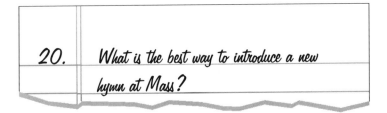

20. What is the best way to introduce a new hymn at Mass?

Prepare before you present the hymn to the assembly. Analyze the hymn to note phrases that repeat. For example, the first and third lines might be the same or similar while the second and fourth are the same or similar. This structure might be put, "A B A B." Reveal this structure to the assembly by informing them that the hymn has only two melodies, the first one, the second one, the first one again, and then the second one again.

Encourage everyone in the assembly to follow the melody line of the new hymn in the hymnal. This basic visual tool is an aid even to those who insist they don't read music. Keep in mind that we don't teach people in three minutes how to read music. We are teaching people in three-minute segments over a lifetime how to watch melody lines, meditate on a sung text, and stretch their boundaries a little further by learning a new piece of music. The cantor sings one phrase line and then asks the assembly to watch the hymnal and sing what they heard. The cantor moves on to the next line, sings it, and asks the assembly to sing what they see and hear. Sing the whole hymn through and have the assembly repeat it.

The first three times you use the hymn in the liturgy, do not have the choir sing choral parts until you hear the assembly sing the melody confidently. The choir is there to facilitate the assembly's song, and once the people are confidently singing the hymn, then the choir can embellish what the assembly sings.

21. What is the best way to introduce a new song that is not a hymn?

Songs such as "I Am the Bread of Life" do not always follow the tight structure of hymnody. If you were to teach it, you would teach only the refrain, phrase by phrase. Once the assembly sang the refrain confidently and heard a cantor or choir singing the verses eight or nine times, you could teach the verses line by line.

Songs with lines that do not repeat are said to be "through-composed." They are more difficult for an assembly to learn all at once and require practice each time they are used over the first year. Repeating them every other week or so also helps to commit the song to memory.

It is good practice to repeat a song or hymn three or four weeks in a row, considering you pay attention to the liturgical year.

22. What parts of the Mass do we have to sing?

Our bishops wrote two fine documents on liturgical music, *Music in Catholic Worship* and *Liturgical Music Today*, which present discussions on the parts of the liturgy we need to sing.

The acclamations to sing include the psalm, the Gospel acclamation, the acclamations during the eucharistic prayer (Holy, memorial acclamation, Amen), and the fraction rite.

Plan music for the entrance procession and the communion procession. The song for the entrance procession gets the assembly ready for the word of God and the liturgical season of the year. It creates unity among the people, who begin as a crowd of strangers and transform into a community of believers, brothers and sisters in Christ. It also accompanies the movement of ministers in the opening procession. St. John Chrysostom described the power of the entrance song, which in his day consisted of psalms set to music:

> As soon as the singing of the psalm begins, it regroups the dispersed voices in unity, it gathers them all together in a harmonious canticle. Young and old, rich and poor, women and men…we all sing a single melody…. The prophet speaks, we all respond, together we form a single choir…. The inequality that exists in the world is laid aside, all form a single choir, all voices are of equal worth, earth imitates heaven (as quoted by Diess, *Visions of Liturgy* 122).

During the communion procession, the song speaks of the action in which the people engage: unity in the Eucharist. Throughout Catholic history, we have used psalms with antiphons for these processions so that the music accompanies the action and ceases when the action is complete. As a result, hymns may not be the best choice for these processions because the message of the hymn is shaped within the entire hymn. Stopping in the middle of a hymn may destroy the message within it.

Plan to sing the psalm every Sunday. Musicians can choose between a seasonal psalm or the psalm of the day for the Sunday assembly.

The assembly can sing ordinary chants such as the Lamb of God, the Gloria, or the Lord Have Mercy. However, singing these chants requires careful planning. For example, if the assembly sings an opening hymn, the Gloria, and the Lord Have Mercy before the opening prayer, the rite is overloaded. Because the goal of the Introductory Rites is to be ready for the word of God, the assembly should not sing three times before the opening prayer. A thoughtful planner would choose the opening hymn or the Gloria or the Lord Have Mercy as the one song during the Introductory Rites. The other two texts would be spoken. For example, during Ordinary Time, sing the opening hymn and speak the other two texts; during Easter time, sing only the Gloria; and during Lent, sing only the Lord Have Mercy.

Consider supplementary songs such as music for the presentation of gifts, the hymn of thanksgiving after communion, and the recessional. A singing assembly might accompany the action of presenting the gifts, but this music could instead be an instrumental or a setting that a choir might offer (tailored to the length of the rite). A "recessional song" was never an official part of the dismissal rite (see MCW 73 and GIRM 123–125). As a result, as a final act of unity, it makes sense to invite the assembly to remain standing after communion and sing a song or hymn of unity (GIRM 121). We will look at the details in Question 51.

23. *What does it mean that we should use the musical, liturgical, and pastoral judgment to choose music for the liturgy?*

When musicians consider a piece of music for the liturgy, they judge whether the piece is worthy to be introduced into the assembly's repertoire. That musical judgment determines whether the piece is well crafted and worthy of use for a lifetime. Connected to that is the liturgical judgment, which helps musicians to discern the appropriateness of the piece of music in relation to the rite. The music must be able to serve the rite and enable the assembly to express its faith. (As a result, the five-movement Masses of the past, which conflict with the assembly's role or the purpose of the rite, are preserved in concert halls. We no longer stop the liturgy in order to listen to a choir sing a Gloria or Credo or silence the assembly while a group sings the Holy.) It is the proper role of the assembly to sing. It is the proper role of liturgical music to serve the rite and accompany its flow. (See GIRM 19, LMT 52, and MCW 30–38.)

The pastoral judgment is made with the musical and liturgical judgments. Every effective liturgy team member operates with the musical-liturgical-pastoral judgment working to balance each perspective so that all three effectively function at the same time. To achieve this balance requires a dialogue among team members (music leader, presider, liturgy director, liturgy committee), who hold the vision of the liturgy in sync with the universal church.

Here is a list of questions a team might consider for this multi-faceted judgment:

- Have all the means possible been used to promote the singing and responding of the assembly at each appropriate moment in the liturgy?
- Has the assembly been carefully and thoughtfully prepared to actively participate in the rite and the music? Do they know what is required of them?
- Does the music chosen help the people to express their cultural and social characteristics, their age, and their educational abilities freely within particular rites of the liturgy?
- Do all leaders of the liturgy know what is expected of them at each part in the liturgy so the liturgy will flow as one continuous prayer?
- Is the music fun to sing?

The musical-liturgical-pastoral judgment requires team members to balance the factors that go into the judgment so that no one element remains in opposition to the other.

24.	*Some of us think we can practice before Mass, but others say we shouldn't. What should musicians do before the Mass begins?*

Musicians should warm up in a space other than the church (not to practice music but to do vocal warm-ups). They should be in place in church for the prelude fifteen minutes before the liturgy begins to settle themselves and to focus on the ministry they are about to begin.

Because singing involves the whole body, the singer needs appropriate rest and careful warm-up. The vocal chords need lubrication, which is why singers need to be encouraged to drink water in the morning to hydrate the voice and the body and to avoid coffee, tea, and milk. Musicians need to eat at least an hour before a warm-up to have energy to sing (don't skip breakfast!).

Once they gather before the liturgy, the group of musicians should exercise the muscles in the face, the tongue, the neck, and the torso. They need to wake up the diaphragm and exercise it, too. The music director can help singers to exercise their voice muscles with a gentle vocal warm-up. The most important element in a vocal warm-up is breathing. Singers must breathe freely and deeply when they sing. There are many exercises to help musicians achieve this. They need exercises to help them focus their sound, to place resonation well in their facial mask, and to exercise articulation. This kind of warm-up should take about twenty minutes.

If the group or individual singer does any singing before the liturgy, it is to exercise the sound, not to practice music. All of this, by the way, should happen in a warm-up room—not in church, where people are greeting one another and praying before the liturgy begins.

If there are instrumentalists, they should also warm up in a separate room using a tuning device. They need time to warm up the instrument so the instrument will stay in tune.

In each case, the time before the liturgy should not be a time to practice lines or review a melody. All of that should be done at a rehearsal.

25. *Is it appropriate for the cantor to ask the assembly to welcome the priest, lectors, and communion ministers before the liturgy begins or to invite the assembly to "...help me greet Father N. with our opening hymn, N.?"*

No. This statement suggests that the assembly is in the position of a passive audience, there to extol the ministry of a few. It also suggests that the assembly sings for the benefit of these few ministers involved in a procession. This is not the purpose of music in the liturgy.

The opening song is the action of every person in the assembly (including those processing in). It gathers their voices into one, thus changing a group of strangers or individuals into a community of brothers and sisters united in song. Song assists "the assembled believers to express and share the gift of faith that is within them and to nourish and strengthen their interior commitment of faith" (MCW 23).

It is appropriate to speak less and simply say something like, "Together, let us sing number 223, 'The City of God.'"

> **26.** *Sometimes, the song or hymn we choose for a procession in the liturgy goes longer than the procession. For example, should the gathering song or hymn stop when the priest arrives at the chair?*

Until this century, the practice of our tradition was that we sang psalm texts during the processions (entrance procession, procession of gifts, and communion procession). It was possible to stop after a verse when the procession ended without disturbing the meaning of the psalm.

In recent decades, we have been using psalms, refrain-verse songs, or metrical hymns (e.g., "Jesus Christ Is Risen Today") during the gathering procession. *Liturgical Music Today* says that if a hymn is used during the opening procession, it is appropriate to allow "the progression of text and music…to play out its course and achieve its purpose musically and poetically" (19). The same article, however, asserts that metrical hymns may not be appropriate for the presentation of gifts procession because the music "should not extend past the time necessary for the ritual." There is an inconsistency in these two statements. For one procession it seems all right to use the whole hymn even though the procession is complete. For another, the hymn should stop because the procession is over.

Some liturgical musicians consider the statements from LMT a compromise written to accommodate recent practice of using hymnody in the liturgy. The belief is that the statement does not take into consideration the centuries-old practice of using the psalm for this procession.

There is a place for hymnody in the liturgy. If we follow the idea that the rite determines the form of music we use to accompany the rite (*Music in Catholic Worship* 23), then we might not use hymns for processions during Mass, including the opening procession. We would use hymns with psalm texts to sing the psalm of the day or season or to sing thanksgiving after communion. These are two times in the liturgy when the rite is the action of singing. Hymnody works very well as the hymn of thanksgiving after communion when the whole assembly stands to sing together. Some hymns or songs which tell a story should not be interrupted if we hope to use it to catechize the assembly. These two times (the psalm and the hymn of thanksgiving) in the liturgy allow the time to sing a story.

However, in his recent book, *Visions of Liturgy and Music for a New Century*, Father Lucien Diess says that focusing the purpose of the gathering rite on the priest's procession projects a clerical vision of church. His view is that the presider's role is to manage himself according to what the community needs and does. The presider's constant concern is whether the people are participating fully in the liturgy at all times. At this point in the liturgy, the presider is aware that the entrance song fulfills a ministerial need: to gather the assembly spiritually as a unified family acclaiming Christ. The presider, with the music minister, monitors how long it takes to create a celebrating community. If it is one verse or six, the music functions for the sake of the assembly, not the presider.

Obviously, there are differing views about the length of the song for the procession. Our role is to consider the purpose of the gathering song, which, the *General Instruction of the Roman Missal* says, is "to open the celebration, intensify the unity of the gathered people, lead their thoughts to the mystery of the season or feast, and accompany the procession of priest and ministers" (25).

The GIRM is the first document written to describe how to celebrate the Mass. A further reflection (*Music in Catholic Worship*), written by the American Catholic Bishops, reminds us that the entrance song is part of the Introductory Rites of the Mass (44):

> The parts preceding the liturgy of the word, namely, the
> entrance, greeting, penitential rite, Kyrie, Gloria, and
> opening prayer or collect, have the character of
> introduction and preparation. The purpose of these rites is
> to help the assembled people become a worshiping

community and to prepare them for listening to God's Word and celebrating the Eucharist (GI 24). Of these parts the entrance song and the opening prayer are primary. All else is secondary.

All of this information can help us to make an informed decision about the approach we take for our assembly. Keep in mind that the active participation of the assembly is the goal to be considered before any other goal.

27. What are the processions in the liturgy?

There are three basic processions in the liturgy: the gathering procession, the procession of gifts to the altar, and the communion procession.

Early in church history, the people (and later, the choir) sang psalms during these moments in the liturgy. We called them the introit, the offertory verse, and the communion antiphon. In the decades just prior to the Second Vatican Council, the texts of these had been reduced to verses, remnants of the practice of singing the psalms during these processions in earlier times.

Today, we recover the practice of singing during the processions. We do not cut the text of the psalm to an antiphon only (as we did prior to the restoration of the liturgy) but use as much of the psalm text as needed to accompany the rite. For example, prior to the Second Vatican Council, singing a psalm for the gathering procession lasted as long as the procession lasted. When the people were in place, the music stopped. Today, we can still use the verses in a psalm so the assembly's song lasts for a very long procession or a very short procession. The same is true for the use of psalms in the processions during the presentation of gifts and communion.

28. Should we sing the Lord Have Mercy?

The Lord Have Mercy can be spoken at times and sung at other times depending on the way the Introductory Rites are shaped for a particular season. For example, during the Easter season (Easter Vigil through the feast of Pentecost) you might use the sprinkling rite instead of the penitential rite. During the sprinkling, we take blessed water from the baptismal font and we remember our baptism, our call to minister. On the other hand, during the season of Lent, the presider and assembly might sing form B of the penitential rite using the Kyrie or "Lord have mercy" as a sung response. In this case, it would be possible to use it as the opening song. Why do I suggest this?

During the restoration of the liturgy, members of the Second Vatican Council were aware that in the Introductory Rites there were three songs before the opening prayer: the entrance song, the Kyrie, and the Gloria. Because the *Constitution on the Sacred Liturgy* asserted that the rites should be short, clear, and unencumbered by useless repetition, the presence of three songs before the Liturgy of the Word posed a problem. They sought a solution to this problem through liturgical research and debate.

The Kyrie was originally the response to prayers of intercession. It was used for evening prayer after the psalms and before the final Lord's Prayer. The church began to use the phrase as a response to the prayers of the faithful in the Mass around the fifth century in the Eastern Catholic Church (Antioch). In the sixth century, the practice was transplanted to the West (Rome), where it was also used as a response to the prayers of the faithful. When prayers of intercession were incorporated into the eucharistic prayer, the formula was separated and the Kyrie moved to the Introductory Rites. Josef Jungmann, SJ, tells us that there are instances in history when the Kyrie litany was substituted for the opening psalm (or song) (333–345).

During the Council, there was a debate over whether to keep the Kyrie in the Introductory Rites. Some scholars recovered ways the Kyrie was used previously and they suggested moving it back to the response of the prayers of the faithful. Others asserted there was no need for a penitential rite because the community prayed the great prayer of reconciliation, the Lord's Prayer, before communion. The group came up with two options for how to handle the Kyrie when there is an opening song: the Kyrie could be spoken (instead of sung) after the Confiteor, thus eliminating another "song" in the Introductory Rites, or the presider would speak tropes followed by a spoken Kyrie (that is, form B of the penitential rite, which is a new invention).

So that we don't sing two songs before the opening prayer, the Council produced the option of speaking the penitential rite text.

29. Why do we sometimes say and sometimes sing the Gloria?

As part of the Introductory Rites, the Gloria was one of three songs the Second Vatican Council had to grapple with. (See Question 28.) If the assembly sang the opening song, the Gloria, and the Kyrie, there was a duplication of opening songs before the opening prayer.

The leaders debated over moving the Gloria to a place right after communion and the Lord Have Mercy to the response of the prayers of the faithful (where it originated). These ideas were too much for some leaders who had not studied the history of liturgy, so they came to a compromise. Although the Gloria is a hymn that has been sung for centuries, they came up with the idea of speaking the hymn text so the opening song would not be duplicated. However, speaking the Gloria, a hymn of praise, is out of place. It's like going to a birthday party and speaking the birthday song instead of singing it.

Historically, prior to the sixth century, the Introductory Rites in the Church of Rome consisted mostly of singing a psalm and chanting or reciting an opening prayer. Later, the Gloria was introduced as a beautiful hymn from the Liturgy of the Hours of the Syrian and Byzantine rite (Eastern Catholic church.) Like the Kyrie, the Gloria was not created for the Mass. It was one among many festive hymns the people sang, a song of thanksgiving. It was used in Evening Prayer and on occasion in the Mass. By the seventh century, it was used in the pope's Mass and eventually in other Masses. The presider turned to intone the Gloria for the people to sing. By the twelfth century, only the choir sang the Gloria.

As a result, in the early 1960s, the choir sang the opening song (introit), the Gloria, and the Kyrie before the opening prayer (collect) in the High Mass. Then the *Constitution on the Sacred Liturgy* said that the "rites should be marked by a noble simplicity; they should be short, clear, and unencumbered by useless repetitions..." (34). Then, the sacramentary of 1969 said that the purpose of the Introductory Rites was to unify the people into a community and prepare them to listen to the word of God and celebrate the Eucharist.

Theologians of post-Vatican II years such as Ralph Kiefer, John Baldovin, and Lucien Diess have followed the discussion of the liturgy committee of the Second Vatican Council that shaped the Introductory Rites of today. They, like the council leaders, refer to the structure of the Introductory Rites of the early church, in which there was a song, the sign of the cross and greeting, followed by the opening prayer. Their research concluded that the Kyrie had been used as a response to intercessory prayer. The Gloria, as a hymn of praise and thanksgiving, had been used as a gathering hymn in Mass, or after communion, and during the vespers liturgy. Today, these writers suggest a seasonal use of the "three songs" of the Introductory Rites. The Kyrie might be the entrance song during Lent, and the Gloria the entrance song during Christmas and Easter seasons. Of course, both would replace a hymn or psalm for the opening song.

When there is a sung gathering song, do not follow with a sung Kyrie and a sung Glory to God. This overloads the Introductory Rites.

30. *What do you do when you've planned to lead a sung Gloria but during Mass Father forgets?*

The choir and instrumentalists may have practiced the Gloria for weeks. However, interrupting the flow of the liturgy to remind Father over the microphone or starting the Gloria over the opening prayer so the group can do the Gloria is missing the point. It is more important that Catholics celebrate the liturgy than witness a moment of chaos between the presider and music leader. Keep a whole-picture perspective. There will be other times of the year when the musicians will be able to lead the Gloria again. The liturgy is continuing, so the music ministry must continue also. When it happens during Mass, give up your plan to sing the Gloria, and follow the presider.

Later, ask for an appointment with the presider during the week to review with him the order of the Introductory Rites. If he forgot about the Gloria, ask if there is a way you can help him to remember it in the future.

31. *Why do we sing the psalm?*

The introduction to the lectionary tells us that the responsorial should be sung (20). It continues: "The singing of the psalm, or even of the response alone, is a great help toward understanding and meditating on the psalm's spiritual meaning" (21).

Psalms are sung prayer. With the psalms, we praise and worship God for all wonderful gifts in life, and we offer thanksgiving. We pray prayers of petition, prayers to grieve our losses, and prayers to ask God's presence during suffering. Singing the psalm is a tradition that reaches back to the time of King David, who, along with his court, is credited with their composition.

We sing the psalms at Mass as a response to the first reading. We give thanks and praise because the Scripture proclaims that which is fulfilled in our hearing. Christ is present in his word when the word is proclaimed. We sing refrains made from psalms to help us memorize some of the psalms of the Bible.

We sing them also because song suspends thought. When a word is set to music, that word is suspended for the ear to hear, the heart to savor, and the brain to memorize. When a prayer text is set to a worthy melody, it supports one who is praying in time of need, "This is the day the Lord has made..." (Ps 118) or in time of trial, "Be with me Lord, when I am in trouble" (Ps 91).

Psalms have always been part of the liturgy. We have used them for prayer and processions of various kinds.

32. How should the psalm be sung?

Psalms can be sung in a variety of ways. They are set in the metrical style, that is, like a hymn (Ps 23: "My Shepherd Will Supply My Need," Text: Psalm [22] 23, Isaac Watts, Tune: RESIGNATION, CMD); in refrain-verse style (Ps 91: "Be With Me Lord," Haugen, GIA); with formula tones (such as J. Gelineau, GIA); or through-composed, in which very little of the music is repeated (Ps 128, R. Wetzler, Augsburg).

Because psalms can be set in these various styles, the music leader must consider the capabilities of the assembly with whom he or she works before choosing the psalm.

If you had a hymn with a psalm text, the assembly could sing the whole setting with no part repeated. Many hymns paraphrase psalms. I don't know of any that uses the very text of a psalm, which is difficult to do because the structure of psalm texts is not as rigidly defined as the hymn structure.

In the refrain-verse style, most often used today, the assembly sings a memorized refrain and the choir or cantor sings the verses.

With formula tones the assembly learns an opening and closing refrain and the cantor or choir sings verses. Sometimes, the refrain is sung after each verse.

The through-composed form is used least often because it requires only a soloist or choir to sing and displaces the active role of the assembly.

Psalms can be sung in these various ways. The question is how a particular form will enable active participation of the assembly and help them to know and memorize psalms. The way they sing the psalm should be beautiful, inviting, and memorable.

33. *We can't understand the words of the responsorial psalm when the cantor or choir sings. What can we do?*

Understanding the words of the psalm is as important as understanding the words the lector proclaims in the first and second readings.

If you cannot understand the cantor, check with those around you to see if they are experiencing the same difficulty. Make certain you consult people of different ages. If they report that they can understand the cantor or choir well, you might consider concentrating harder on the cantor or choir sound. If you still have a problem, go to the cantor or choir director after the liturgy and introduce yourself. Simply report your problem and ask if there is something he or she might suggest to help you. A question asked in gentleness and kindness reaps many benefits. You might feel frustrated but keep in mind that no one likes to deal with an aggressive or angry person. (The worst time to approach a leader is during the last fifteen minutes before the liturgy.)

In any case, talk with the cantor or choir director well after the liturgy. Ask for an appointment to talk about your concern. Be prepared to be part of the solution, which might mean sponsoring a workshop with an expert on diction.

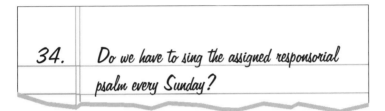

34. *Do we have to sing the assigned responsorial psalm every Sunday?*

The psalm between the first and second readings is chosen for us in the lectionary every Sunday. A "responsorial psalm" helps us to respond in song and meditation to the Scripture of the day. However, we can plan a seasonal psalm instead of the assigned psalm for the day. In the introduction to the lectionary, we learn about this option:

> But to make it easier for the people to join in the response to the psalm, the Order of Readings lists certain other texts of psalms and responses that have been chosen according to the various seasons or classes of saints. Whenever the psalm is sung, these texts may replace the text corresponding to the reading (89).

This same point is reiterated in *Music in Catholic Worship*,

> Since most groups cannot learn a new response every week, seasonal refrains are offered in the lectionary itself.... Other psalms and refrains may also be used...and are selected in harmony with the liturgical season, feast, or occasion (63).

We can use the seasonal psalm option to build the parish psalm repertoire. The long term goal would be to build a repertoire of psalms throughout the liturgical year that can be added to a master list of psalms the people know by heart. Once the master list is large enough, the parish could take the next step: to sing a well-crafted psalm setting for each week's psalm and use the psalms for other processions and rites in the liturgy.

35. Are we supposed to sing the Easter and Pentecost sequences?

The sequence is optional except on Easter Sunday and Pentecost, according to the *General Instruction of the Roman Missal*. Throughout history, the text was sung, not recited, in the Mass of the day. It is sung after the second reading and before the Gospel acclamation. Although it was developed by cantors and choirs, today it can be sung by all. To understand this further, let's review its development.

The sequence began during a period of history when the Roman liturgy was influenced by the French people (800 AD). During this time, the cantor improvised a plainchant melody that began with the closing note of the Gospel Alleluia (originally, the sequence occurred after the Alleluia instead of before it). Others memorized the melodies of gifted improvisationalists. Imagine one singer continuing the last syllable and last note and making up a new melody while singing only the last syllable of the Alleluia. This was called the *jubilis*.

Around the year 900 AD, short texts appeared under the melodies with one syllable per note. The text was called the "sequence." Gradually, the sequence after the Gospel acclamation disappeared. By the year 1000 AD, the texts were organized into verse and strophes with rhyme. Eventually, the church developed about five thousand sequences. Today we sing the sequence texts as a hymn for devotional prayer such as the Stations of the Cross (*Stabat Mater*, "At the Cross her station keeping"), as a sequence or hymn of praise on Easter or during the Easter season (*Victimae paschali laudes*, "To the Paschal Victim"), as a sequence or hymn of praise on Pentecost, the final day of Easter (*Veni, Sancte Spiritus*, "Come Holy Spirit, Come"), or as a hymn of praise on Trinity Sunday (*Te Deum Laudeamus*, "Holy God, we praise Thy Name.") (See Josef A. Jungmann, SJ, *The Mass of the Roman Rite*, vol. 1.)

There are three sequences in today's lectionary; one is optional. We have the Easter and Pentecost sequence texts; the optional sequence is that of the feast of the Body and Blood of Christ.

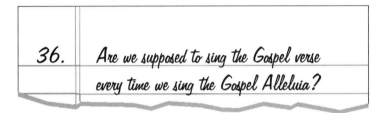

36. *Are we supposed to sing the Gospel verse every time we sing the Gospel Alleluia?*

The introduction to the lectionary says that "the *Alleluia* or the verse before the gospel must be sung and during it all stand. It is not to be sung only by the cantor who intones it or by the choir, but by the whole congregation together" (23). This suggests that either the Alleluia or the verse is sung. This statement also appears in two places in the *General Instruction of the Roman Missal*.

The verses are used in liturgies in which the deacon has placed the word of God on the altar during the opening procession. It is enthroned there until the Gospel acclamation begins. The Alleluia-verse-Alleluia is the ritual music the assembly sings during the procession to the ambo.

The GIRM describes what happens during the Gospel acclamation when there is a deacon. He assists the presider as he prepares the incense, then bows for his blessing, joins at the altar the acolytes, who bear lighted candles, picks up the Book of the Gospels (separate from the book containing the other readings), and processes it to the ambo. There, he greets the people and incenses the Gospel. The Gospel verse sung with the Alleluia completes the ritual.

In most cathedrals, this procession is substantial; in the local parish, it is a short walk, often requiring ten or fewer steps. Parishes should take care not to prolong the Gospel acclamation beyond the time it takes to arrive at the ambo. As a result, the Alleluia without the verse may be long enough for the procession.

37. Should we sing the prayers of the faithful?

The prayers of the faithful are sung. They may be spoken, too. However, if they are sung, the ministers involved need to be able to clearly articulate the prayers through a sung melody. This must be rehearsed carefully so that when it is sung it is prayerful.

One might use a sung setting during a season such as Advent or Christmas or Lent or Easter. There could be chanted intercessions each week. The assembly sings the response, thus making the dialogue in song and prayer complete.

In the prayers of the faithful, we pray for the world, the church, for local community issues, and the dead. The prayers may reflect the Scripture of the day, the week's news, and events of the praying community. (See GIRM 45 and Lucien Diess's *Visions of Liturgy* 180.)

38. Who sings the prayers of the faithful?

The presider chants the prayer of introduction, the deacon (or cantor if there is no deacon) chants the prayer texts (GIRM 132), and the assembly sings the response to the prayers of the faithful.

When there is a choir, they may embellish the assembly's response with three-or four-part harmony around the assembly's melody.

---

39. *Do we have to sing the Holy at every Mass?*

The document *Liturgical Music Today* clearly says that the Holy is one among other acclamations that are "preeminent sung prayers of the eucharistic liturgy" (17). When we sing the Holy, memorial acclamation, Amen, Lamb of God, psalm, and Gospel acclamation (which must always be sung), our prayer is more effective. In fact, the document says we should sing the Holy and other acclamations even at daily Mass.

---

40. *We want to do the latest setting of a sung eucharistic prayer. How do we get the priest to sing?*

Begin by asking the parish priest if he *wants* to sing or learn to sing the eucharistic prayer. It is fair to invite him and allow him the room to choose to sing it or not. If he chooses not to, you can still use the acclamations of the musical setting of the prayer.

If he chooses to try, you need to prepare well in advance so he can become comfortable with the musical setting. He needs time practicing at the altar with the microphone. He needs to practice singing while using the bread and wine and all the gestures he normally uses during the eucharistic prayer. He needs to decide whether he will sing it from memory or from a musical score, which means he will need a score in a presentable binder. Plan out the details with him.

Working with a person's voice is an intimate experience. The present-day parish priest needs to practice singing with a musician who is willing to take time to build a trusting relationship. The two of you are a team.

Learning to sing must begin before the person is a priest. Some seminary formation programs have full-time vocal coaches on staff. (If your local diocesan seminary doesn't, ask why and encourage the administration to get one. Remember, you are the source of their funding.) Seminarians going through formation should be required to take voice lessons. A requirement like this helps candidates for the priesthood prepare well to lead the sung liturgy.

When we regularly sang Gregorian chant in the pre-Vatican II church, we taught our seminarians how to read chant notes and how to sing them. It was required. Today, we need to recover this practice of teaching seminarians how to read liturgical music and sing the liturgy (CLS 115).

It is possible that our future priests, who are now singing in the assembly as children, will approach this ministry with a fresh attitude about singing.

41. *How should we choose acclamations for the eucharistic prayer — the Holy, memorial acclamation, and Amen?*

Think of the eucharistic prayer as one grand prayer before the meal. As an example, look at Eucharistic Prayer IV, which has its own preface. The prayer begins with the dialogue, then the preface, followed by the first acclamation, the Holy; then it continues with the anamnesis (which is a remembering of salvation history), the calling of the Holy Spirit upon the offerings, the institution narrative, the memorial acclamation, prayers that are like intercessions, the doxology, and the Amen. When we view the eucharistic prayer this way, we can see that the acclamations are part of one prayer.

As a result, the Holy, memorial acclamation, and Amen should reflect one musical style expressing a unity in sound. Choosing acclamations written by three different composers with three different musical ideas can break apart our understanding and celebration of the eucharistic prayer.

Choose acclamations written in a Mass setting by one composer, or write a memorial acclamation and Amen using musical ideas from the Holy. By their choice of music, liturgical musicians can help the assembly experience the prayer as one prayer as opposed to a series of prayers. We are musicians and catechists.

42.	*Is it okay to teach a new Holy, memorial acclamation, and Amen to the assembly by rote? We don't have the new music in our hymnal.*

It is all right as long as you have purchased (not copied) the music for the choir and obtained the permission for use with the assembly. Even though the assembly might not have a printed copy, they are still singing the composer's song. As a matter of justice, the composer deserves payment for her or his work in order that he or she may gain financial support to continue writing.

Almost every publishing company or copyright owner has guidelines for this kind of use. In all fairness to the composer, take the time to call the publisher and make arrangements.

43. Can a singer or choir group solo the Lord's Prayer?

We pray the Lord's Prayer immediately after we finish the eucharistic prayer. The Lord's Prayer begins the communion rite. We begin this rite when each person gathers in one voice asking for our daily bread and for forgiveness of sins before we receive the Body and Blood of Jesus in communion. It is one prayer in the liturgy we all speak together.

It is not appropriate to mute the assembly and require them to listen to one person offer our petition and ask for forgiveness. Nor is it appropriate to replace the assembly's prayer with a singing choir. These actions rob the community of full, conscious, and active participation.

44. Why does our liturgy director want us to sing the Lamb of God?

Recall from the discussion in Question 1 that Catholics sing the rites in the liturgy. We sing the litany "Lamb of God" during the rite called "the fraction rite" (cf. GIRM 283). We repeat the acclamation as "often as necessary to accompany the breaking of the bread" and the pouring of wine into cups (GIRM 56e). For centuries, Christians have sung this ancient text from Scripture (Jn 1:29) to sing the fraction rite.

The sung text creates for us a more solemn, proclamatory expression of our faith. As the Body of Christ is held before us broken and torn, we recognize Jesus as the disciples did on the road to Emmaus. We recognize Jesus in the breaking of the bread.

The drama of this moment when we remember Jesus as the Lamb led to the slaughter, whose blood poured out on the earth for us, is heightened as we proclaim, united in song, what we believe: "Jesus, Lamb of God, you take away the sins of the world, have mercy on us." His broken body and poured out blood is evident at this very moment in the Mass.

In today's liturgy, however, it is not appropriate to sing one of the settings of the Lamb of God (Agnus Dei) from a five-movement Mass composed before the Second Vatican Council. Most often these fine works required the liturgy to stop while the choir continued the music and the assembly remained silent. This practice reflected times in liturgical history when the music became predominant over the experience of the rite.

Today's liturgy requires the assembly to sing the rite, and the music stops when the rite is complete. As a result, a "Lamb of God" written in the form of a litany allows the flexibility we need to sing the rite.

45. How should we sing the Lamb of God?

The priest begins to break the consecrated bread apart as the assembly sings, "Lamb of God you take away the sins of the world...." As the communion ministers assist by breaking the bread parts into bite-size pieces and pouring the wine into smaller cups, the cantor leads the Lamb of God acclamation. Each time the acclamation is repeated, the cantor uses other invocations or names for Jesus in place of the phrase "Lamb of God," such as, "Prince of Peace, Cup of Salvation, Son of God, Hope for All." These acclamations aid in our sung and visual meditation on Jesus, whose body is broken for us and whose blood is poured out for our salvation. *Liturgical Music Today* (20) tells us:

> The Lamb of God achieves greater significance at Masses
> when a larger sized eucharistic bread is broken for
> distribution and, when communion is given under both

kinds, chalices must be filled. The litany is prolonged to accompany this action of breaking and pouring (GIRM 56e).

46.   What is the communion rite?

The communion rite begins with the Lord's Prayer and ends with the prayer after communion. Musicians lead the Lamb of God, the song during the communion procession, and the hymn of thanksgiving after communion. The liturgical musician is careful to make the transition musically graceful and prayerful throughout the communion rite.

If the announcements occur before the dismissal, they should be done after the communion prayer so the continuity of the communion rite will be uninterrupted. (See GIRM 123.)

47.   How do musicians help the rites in the communion rite to connect?

The Mass, from beginning to end, is like one tapestry which we weave together. To accomplish this work, we need the assembly of believers, hospitality ministers, communion ministers, lectors, ushers, and music ministers—all who participate—to make one tapestry which tells an important story. Each group has a particular part in the liturgy. When one ministry finishes its function, the rite passes to the next ministry like water flowing in a river.

During the communion rite, the music ministers have the opportunity to unify the rite through music. They can make the music flow from the Lamb of God to the communion procession and to the song of praise.

Because the music is one with the rite, the leader is very attentive to each stage in the action so the music will end at the appropriate time—after the action is complete.

Music ministers work to make the flow of sound move smoothly like water flowing. The communion rite flows from the Lord's Prayer to the fraction rite to the communion procession to the hymn of praise and concludes with the communion prayer.

48.	*The way we move from any one part of the liturgy can be either graceful or jarring. How can I help the musicians and priests to understand how the liturgy flows from one rite to the next?*

In his pastoral letter *Gather Faithfully Together: A Guide for Sunday Mass*, Cardinal Roger Mahony says that every priest and liturgical musician needs to be concerned about the flow of the liturgy. They can help each other at their weekly or monthly planning meetings by talking about each liturgy as a story.

In his book *Modern Liturgy Answers the 101 Most-Asked Questions about Liturgy*, Nick Wagner develops the following concept of the liturgy. He says that the liturgy has a beginning, a middle, and an end. In the Liturgy of the Word, we tell many stories in which God speaks. When God speaks, creation occurs and we are filled with faith. In faith, we respond at the table of the Lord, from which we come into union when we share the Body and Blood of Jesus. Then, we are sent into the world to be the presence of Christ and transform the world.

Both the presider and musician need to imagine the story we tell from its very beginning: from the moment Catholics rise to get ready for the liturgy to the moment the presider dismisses them into the world once again. When the prelude begins, the musicians continue the story begun by those who have assembled and help to focus them to become one in spirit, a community. Every word, song, and gesture from that moment in the liturgy affects how the story continues or is interrupted, how well we become a community of believers. The lector, the communion ministers, the ushers, the musicians, the catechist, and the presider co-preside throughout the storytelling.

The musicians in our parish imagine that there is a baton that is passed from one leader to the next during Sunday liturgy. When the gathering song is finished, the musicians pass the baton to the priest, who leads the opening dialogue with the assembly. When the gathering rite is complete, the priest passes the baton to the lector, who proclaims the Scripture. The lector passes it to the cantor, who leads the psalm dialogue with the assembly. The cantor passes it back to the lector, who proclaims the second reading. After the proclamation, the lector passes it to the priest, who proclaims the Gospel and delivers the homily. And so on throughout the liturgy. The catechist takes the baton during the dismissal of the catechumens; the ushers during the collection. It goes back to the priest for the eucharistic prayer. The communion ministers share it during the fraction rite. During the whole liturgy, we pass the baton from one of these leaders back and forth to the music minister and the priest. If the musicians are not going with the flow of the prayer and the telling of the story, the continuity is broken and the attention of all assembled falls on the individual who "dropped the baton" or broke the flow. Each leader and member of the assembly needs to remain focused on the community's storytelling. In order to do that, a good presiding team learns to be caring and flexible with one another.

When every minister is focused on the story we tell together, everyone can be caught up in the flow of the prayer. The assembly must be actively involved every step of the way.

49.	*At which point in the communion rite should the musicians share in communion?*

Musicians should share in communion after the assembly has received and before the prayer after communion. While the choir or ensemble shares communion, the keyboard player can continue to play the melody of the communion procession song or introduce the melody of the hymn of thanksgiving. When the choir or ensemble returns, the group can continue the instrumental with a flute, guitar or with voices humming the melody and parts of the song while the keyboard person shares.

50.	*We quit scheduling vocal music during communion because the people don't sing anyway. We've been told that is wrong. Why?*

Music ministers are often tempted to respond in a practical way to what they see. However, in this case it is important to ask, "Why does the Roman Missal say the people sing during the communion procession? What is the historical perspective of this practice? What is the spiritual perspective? What other musical forms can be used for the communion procession to make it successful?"

The Roman Missal says that the people sing during the communion procession:

> The General Instruction takes for granted that there will be
> singing…(during the communion rite; see nos. 26, 56, 83,
> 119), certainly in the Sunday celebration of the eucharist (p.
> 14).
>
> During the priest's and the faithful's reception of the
> sacrament the communion song is sung. Its function is to
> express outwardly the communicants' union in spirit by
> means of the unity of their voices, to give evidence of joy
> of heart, and to make the procession to receive Christ's
> body more fully an act of community. The song begins
> when the priest takes the communion and continues for as
> long as seems appropriate while the faithful receive
> Christ's body. But the communion song should be ended in
> good time whenever there is to be a hymn after communion.
>   An antiphon from the *Graduale Romanum* may be also
> be used, with or without the psalm, or an antiphon with
> psalm from *The Simple Gradual* or another suitable song
> approved by the conference of bishops. It is sung by the
> choir alone or by the choir or cantor with the
> congregation (56i).
>
> The communion song is begun while the priest is receiving
> the sacrament (119).

Historically, the Roman Catholic Church has always accompanied the communion procession with music. In his book *The Mass of the Roman Rite*, Rev. Josef A. Jungmann, SJ, said that the communion song appeared in the fourth century, first as a responsorial song (the people had a recurring refrain and the cantor chanted a psalm). Sometimes, the assembled sang an Alleluia refrain after each verse of the psalm. They used psalms like 144 and 33; other texts included Luke 2:14; Matthew 21:9; Psalm 117:26, 27; and Matthew 21:9. These two psalms appeared in the West (Roman) and in the East (Byzantine). He tells us that, "Whereas in the ancient period the communicants themselves as a rule took part in this song, we find in the later sources…that this communion song or one of the communion songs was turned over to the choir" (Jungmann 393).

During this time, choirs began to use texts other than psalms. The choirs sang other texts and hymns during the communion procession. The psalms in the communion procession began to disappear during the tenth century and were barely found in the twelfth century. Catholics participated in the communion song less and less as the church restricted more and more music to the choir (which eventually consisted of male voices only). Only a short psalm verse was sung during the priest's communion.

The communion psalms were moved into a category called post-communion antiphons. Then, when people began to share communion again sometime after 1910, the psalm was still sung after the people's communion. The communion psalm was diminished to a phrase of the psalm that the priest read or the choir sang. It was called the communion verse. (Catholics participated in communion less, and as a result, they used less music to accompany the procession [Jungmann 394–400]). Vatican II helped us to recover what we are meant to do with song during the communion procession—sing it as we process and share communion.

Spiritually, we sing the experience we have in communion so that all of us will be more focused on sharing Christ's Body and Blood in order to become the Body and Blood of Christ, which is then sent out to the world to transform the world.

A music leader might use other musical forms during the communion procession. The most successful is the refrain-verse style used in musical settings of psalms and other songs. The communion processional music is best suited for the assembly when it is sung from memory in refrain-verse style. This takes careful planning and repetition of communion music in order to help the assembly sing by memory. The goal is to sing a song enough times that the assembly sings the refrain by heart.

It is better for the communicant to have his or her hands free to use only for sharing communion. In centuries past, the church used psalms at this particular time to facilitate this action. Although the psalm was sung only by the choir during some periods in church history, now the primary choir, the assembly, sings it.

51. Can we sing a Holy in Latin for a meditation piece after communion?

Within the liturgy itself, Catholics sing the Holy, one of the primary acclamations during the eucharistic prayer. Singing this text is the duty of the assembled.

The Latin Holy or Sanctus was part of a five-movement Mass setting prior to the Second Vatican Council. When it was sung, the liturgy stopped for the duration of its musical setting while the choir sang and the priest and assembly remained passive. Many Latin settings expanded the text by repeating parts of it two or three times before moving onto the next phrase of the Sanctus. The rite adjusted for the sake of the music.

When we restored the liturgy, we set the perspective on the rite. Liturgical music is a servant to the liturgical rite. As a result, the rite remains the primary focus of liturgical musicians as they plan music for the liturgy. They discern how a piece will establish active participation of the assembly in the liturgy, how it will serve the liturgy, how it will contribute to the flow of the liturgy, and how it will form the assembly in its mission as disciples of Christ. "The musical form employed must match its liturgical function" (LMT 11).

The text belongs to the people as their active part in the eucharistic prayer. Using this text otherwise would cause duplication. Because the restoration of the liturgy focused us on not duplicating gesture, text, and song, it would be improper to present the text of this acclamation before, during, or after the liturgy out of context.

There are times in the liturgy when sung prayer is the focus of a rite. *Liturgical Music Today* (10) lists some of those times:

> the song of praise, which may be sung after communion (GIRM 56j); the litany of saints at celebrations of Christian initiation (RCIA 214, Baptism 48)...; the proclamation of

> praise for God's mercy at the conclusion of the rite of reconciliation (*Rite of Penance* 56)....

The time after communion must not be misunderstood. This is a time when, as the *General Instruction of the Roman Missal* states, "a hymn, psalm, or other song of praise may be sung by the entire congregation" (56j). Active participation is our goal above all others (CSL 14). Music after communion was not intended to be used only by the choir to showcase its abilities, nor was it intended to create listening music for a passive audience. Rather, it is a time for silence that everyone participates in or for a song of praise which all who are assembled sing. It is a time for active participation of all assembled.

The five-movement Latin Mass settings, or individual settings, are well suited in settings outside the liturgy where people gather to listen to music for music's sake.

Parts of the five-movement Latin Mass can be used in the liturgy when the assembly sings the text to serve the rite. Generally speaking, music in the liturgy must enhance and engage the baptized in ritual action.

> **52.** *At the neighboring parish, there is no song for the people to sing at the end of Mass. Isn't that improper?*

The *General Instruction of the Roman Missal* states:

> Immediately after the blessing, with hands joined, the priest adds: *Go in the peace of Christ.* ... The priest then kisses the altar, makes the proper reverence with the ministers, and leaves (GIRM 124, 125).

The GIRM also states:

> After communion, the priest and people may spend some time in silent prayer. If desired, a hymn, psalm, or other song of praise may be sung by the entire congregation. ... The concluding rite consists of: a. the priest's greeting and blessing...; b. the dismissal of the assembly (56j, 57).

Nowhere in the *General Instruction* is a closing hymn mentioned beyond the hymn or song the assembly sings after communion.

Music in Catholic Worship refers to this instruction but inserts a suggestion that a song after the dismissal is one possible choice (a suggestion reflecting no previous historical practice). However, it clearly states that if the assembly sings a song of thanksgiving after communion, it advises the use of instrumental or choral music for a song after the dismissal.

Questions From Choir Leaders And Members

> **53.** *I am a volunteer choir director and I want to learn more about what is appropriate to do in the post-Vatican II liturgy. Where do I begin? Are there any summer programs to form me for liturgical music?*

It's great that you wish to do some study.

First, you will want to have a copy of the liturgical documents. Liturgy Training Publications has a collection of the more important documents in one book entitled *The Liturgy Documents: A Parish Resource.* You can access many of the documents I refer to in this book at your local bookstore or directly through the publishers.

You can also go to the internet, where you can search Catholic universities and look up their theology departments. Many have two-week institutes or six-week summer programs in which to participate. You will want to look for courses in liturgical music, the psalms, the structure of the liturgy, or a guided reading of the liturgical documents.

Also check in your local university library for Catholic magazines which have information on these kind of programs. For example, MINISTRY & LITURGY magazine publishes program descriptions of these programs once a year.

You can also order copies of the Roman Missal (the sacramentary) and the lectionary. These are called primary resources.

Authors who write about the liturgy include Josef A. Jungmann, SJ, Mark Searle, Kevin Seasoltz, OSB, Godfrey Diekmann, OSB, Virgil Michel, OSB, Robert Hovda, Gabe Huck, Cardinal Roger Mahony, Kathleen Hughes, RSCJ, Nathan Mitchell, Ed Foley, Capuchin, Sam Torvend, Paul Covino, and Nick Wagner.

Musicians who write about liturgical music include Lucien Diess, SSSp, Michael Joncas, Sue Seid-Martin, Anthony Ruff, OSB, Joseph Gelineau, SJ, Christopher Walker, Kim Kasling,

Marty Haugen, Grayson Warren Brown, Dolores Martinez, Marie Kramer, and Leon C. Roberts.

54.	*Our new pastor and new music director are making us change how we do music to "conform to the church documents on the liturgy." How can we prepare ourselves for a discussion with them?*

To prepare for a discussion, prepare to read and expand your knowledge of what the church teaches regarding liturgy and music. Get a copy of *The Liturgy Documents: A Parish Resource.* Read *The Constitution on the Sacred Liturgy, Music in Catholic Worship,* and *Liturgical Music Today.* (Other helpful documents are listed in the annotated bibliography of this book.) These documents are also published individually.

In *The Constitution on the Sacred Liturgy,* you will read about the Church's universal view on music in the liturgy. It is the first document of the Second Vatican Council. The documents *Music in Catholic Worship* and *Liturgical Music Today* were written by American Catholic bishops who give the parish musician a more detailed description of how to plan music for today's liturgy. These documents contain clarifications and develop the ideas and spirit of *The Constitution on the Sacred Liturgy.*

I also recommend that you read *Environment and Art in Catholic Worship* (published in *The Liturgy Documents*) because it begins with a well-written theology of Catholic worship and the role of the assembly. Next, I recommend *The Milwaukee Symposia for Church Composers: A Ten-Year Report,* published by Liturgical Training Publications. This short document contains a rich reflection of the state of liturgical music up to 1992 with very good recommendations for the future.

As liturgical musicians, you and I must diligently work to implement the vision of music for the liturgy articulated by the Second Vatican Council. We can make beautiful music but we must also judge how well the music promotes active participation in the assembly. That is because active participation in the sung liturgy forms Catholics and grounds all Catholics with the true Christian spirit.

55. *I am a volunteer choir director. How can I get choir members who tend to mumble to sing with clarity and confidence?*

The most important thing a choir member needs is the opportunity to study and practice a piece over time. If the director is giving the group a new piece of music two weeks before it is needed in the liturgy, the singers will be insecure and uncomfortable when they sing it. Long-term practice of a piece gives the singer time to know the text and the music that expresses the text.

The director should be careful not to simply run through the whole choral piece at every practice. It is the director's job to guide the group through a progressive, phrase-by-phrase study each week and to put the phrases together at appropriate stages in the weekly study.

Every time a choir has a rehearsal or sings in a liturgy, they need to be guided through a warm-up session. Appropriate warm-up sessions help the singer to get in touch with the parts of the body which help them to sing with articulation and clarity (see Question 24).

56. *How can we get more people in the choir? We make announcements but no one comes.*

When a liturgical choir maintains its focus on the active participation of the assembly, has fun, enjoys the fellowship and spirituality of its mission, and is good at music making, it attracts new members.

Will a new person feel free to approach your group and find that every person in the choir is hospitable? Few want to join a group who ignores individuals who "hang out" near the choir. Every week, each choir member should be in the habit of looking for these individuals and reaching out to them, introducing yourself and getting to know their names. Is your choir open to inviting new people?

Another way to attract inquirers is to invite parishioners to join just for Christmas rehearsals and sing during the Christmas season. Have a system ready so that each visitor sits with a choir member who guides him or her through the rehearsal. At the end of this rehearsal, have refreshments and goodies ready so each choir member can spend time with the visitors.

Sometimes this method attracts people with fewer musical skills. Be prepared to invite guests to sing melody lines in the choir on the hymns, songs, and acclamations which involve the assembly. You could reserve the choir music for "core choir" members only. The guideline might be that if a person would like to sing parts, she or he may audition for seasonal placement in the choir. That way, the choir director can screen those who have difficulty with pitch and place them around key members who can guide them with melody lines. Others might be invited to join the sections for part-singing. Ask the section leader to reinforce rehearsal accomplishments with newcomers in special sectional meetings. (If you don't have section leaders who can practice with their section at home during the week, why not train some?)

Regarding long-term membership in the choir, hold auditions for choir membership. There are diplomatic ways to assess those with weak musical gifts honestly and to help them to discern their ministry in the parish. Sometimes, required group voice lessons before re-auditioning clarifies their future in music or supports them so they can indeed grow into membership with the choir. Help adults, in particular, experience discernment versus judgment in regard to their skills.

It takes years to build a good liturgical choir. The fortunate element is that people like to stay in parish liturgical choirs. Approach each person with the thought that each person is the presence of Christ whose relationship and presence in the community is essential. And as carriers of Christ's presence ourselves, we do not throw away or disregard relationships and people but rather dignify them and reinforce their call to minister in one way or another in parish life. They may not be suited for music but they may be important ministers of God's word, of basic needs for those in need, or of another ministry in the parish. A choir leader or member is "first a disciple and then a minister" (LMT 64).

57. When can the choir sing without the assembly?

The primary purpose of a liturgical choir is to assume the role of leadership of the Catholic assembly to lead them in "sung prayer, by alternating or reinforcing the sacred song of the congregation, or by enhancing it with the addition of a musical elaboration (*Bishops' Committee on the Liturgy* Newsletter [April 18, 1966])" (MCW 36). This primary purpose should be taken seriously.

There are times when the liturgical choir will sing without the assembly. For example, the choir might sing a prelude before the liturgy or sing during the collection or after the dismissal.

The prelude helps prepare the assembly with the spirit of celebration. The piece might be joyful and energetic, as in Easter, Christmas, Ordinary Time, or funerals (which celebrate the resurrection of the believer). It might be a solemn preparation for the season of Lent or a subdued preparation for an Advent liturgy.

The collection is a time of action for the assembly, who gathers together their resources first in order to share them with those in need and second to share with one another for the maintenance of common parish property. This action is followed by a procession of gifts to the altar. The choir might offer a psalm to reflect this action or a piece written to reflect the season of the church year. Music that takes longer than the action should be reserved for prelude or postlude time in the liturgy.

The GIRM describes the primary purpose of music during the communion procession:

> During the priest's and the faithful's reception of the sacrament the communion song is sung. Its function is to express outwardly the communicants' union in spirit by means of the unity of their voices, to give evidence of joy of heart, and to make the procession to receive Christ's body more fully an act of community. The song begins when the priest takes the communion and continues for as long as seems appropriate while the faithful receive Christ's body. But the communion song should be ended in good time whenever there is to be a hymn after communion (56i).

Whether you plan the hymn of thanksgiving as the final hymn the assembly sings or insert a hymn after the final blessing and dismissal (a practice not described in the GIRM), it is important that the organist, the pianist, or the choir or folk ensemble play or sing jubilant music to accompany the procession out into the world. The assembly has been commissioned to continue the mission of Christ ("Go in peace to love and serve the Lord"), and music can energize the Christians. They go forth energized once again to transform the world into the kingdom.

58. *Why can't we sing Christmas carols during Advent?*

Although in the dominant culture in America we hear Christmas carols four weeks or more before Christmas, in the Catholic church, we are not yet celebrating Christmas. We do not use Christmas songs during this time. The season of Advent has a unique story to tell and its color, mood, and music reflect the story of how our ancestors waited for the Messiah. All of our music is focused on the story of Advent.

Christmas carols may be used starting at the vigil Mass of Christmas, December 24, until the feast of the Baptism of the Lord, a moveable feast in January. Christmas, for us, lasts about three weeks.

59. *Is it all right to photocopy extra copies of music for the choir, especially if our parish is "poor"?*

It is unjust and illegal to copy music without permission of the publisher or unpublished composer.

Music may be copied with permission from the publisher or copyright owner for purposes of music study in an educational setting such as a music theory class or a workshop on liturgical music. With permission and a fee, some music can be copied for the choir and assembly.

A warning: A choir director might reason that because the parish has the license to copy music for the assembly only, he or she can copy music with parts for use with a choir. Take a good look at your reprint license statement. Many publishers do not allow this. It would be a good idea to check with the publisher to clarify this point.

According to the Library of Congress Copyright Office, a copyright is*

> a form of protection provided by the laws of the United States to the authors of "original works of authorship" including literary, dramatic, musical, artistic, and certain other intellectual works. It is illegal for anyone to violate any of the rights provided by the copyright code to the owner of copyright.... Copyright protection subsists from the time the work is created in fixed form.

Works which can be copyrighted include literary works and *musical works, including any accompanying words...*

> A work that is created on or after January 1, 1978, is automatically protected from the moment of its creation and is ordinarily given a term enduring for the author's life plus an additional 50 years after the author's death.

> Works created before January 1, 1978 (are valid for)...28 years from the date it was secured. During the last (28th) year of the first term, the copyright was eligible for renewal. The current copyright law has extended the renewal term from 28 to 47 years for copyrights that were subsisting on January 1, 1978, making these works eligible for a total term of protection of 75 years.

> For works first published on and after March 1, 1989, use of the copyright notice is optional...

> This protection is available to both published and unpublished works...[and] gives the owner of copyright the exclusive right to do and to authorize others to do the following:

> • To reproduce the copyrighted work in copies...;

> • To prepare derivative works based upon the copyrighted work;

---

* The following quoted material is from The Copyright Act. For further information contact: Library of Congress; Copyright Office; Publications Section, LM-455; 101 Independence Avenue, S.E.; Washington, DC 20559-6000; http://lcweb.loc.gov/copyright/circs/circ1.html

- To distribute copies or phonorecords of the copyrighted work to the public...;

- To display the copyrighted work publicly....

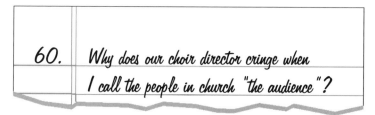

60. Why does our choir director cringe when I call the people in church "the audience"?

The people who gather for the liturgy actively participate in the total action of the liturgy. It is not proper for them to sit waiting for someone to do something to them or to please them.

In a theater, the people who gather remain passive while the actors present the story. They are spectators who are seated and watch a handful of players present the action. They respond with emotion, interest, or support.

In the liturgy, the people are not to be passive but active. They are the players who proclaim the story in the Word and enact the story in the Eucharist. They are the players in the story engaged in gesture, movement, and procession—action. They carry on the ancient dialogue in the liturgy which they grow to know by heart. The people of God join together to pray.

The Second Vatican Council carefully defined the role of the people, saying that everyone should be conscious and active and ready to participate fully in the liturgy (see *Constitution on the Sacred Liturgy* 14). Baptism has made it our right and *our duty* to participate fully.

An assembly of believers is not an audience. In his pastoral letter *Gather Faithfully Together*, Cardinal Roger Mahony put it simply:

> People do not want to be entertained and passive. They want to become energized in the hard but delightful work of liturgy, praising and thanking God, remembering the liberating deeds of God, interceding for all the world. These desires are most clear when people enter into the spirit of the Eucharistic Prayer and share in the Paschal

Banquet. What a witness to the Spirit-inspired work of Vatican II! (25).

61.	*We want to turn up the sound system so everyone can hear us. Can a music group ever have the sound system turned up too loud?*

A music ministry group can have the sound system too loud. What happens when it is too loud? The assembly can get "lazy" and shed their responsibility for full and active participation. They allow the full sound from the system to fill the room. Because of the loud sound, people in the assembly become passive and in some situations regress either to individualistic prayer or to visiting with their neighbors.

Sometimes, members of the assembly complain that they can't hear the group. Use this teachable moment to catechize. The assembly should hear only the cantor. After that, the group's sound must blend in with the assembly until what is mostly heard is the assembly.

Prior to twentieth-century technology, churches were crafted so that the assembly could hear the word, the homily, and the music. That is why some of our older churches are acoustically live. Priests were trained to project their voices to proclaim the word and preach, and choirs were large so they would be heard.

With the introduction of the sound system, the acoustics in some of our newer churches changed. Now, almost every church has a sound system.

We liturgical musicians need to be careful when we use amplified sound. The louder the sound system, the less the assembly will freely sing because the music ministry fills the church with amplified sound. As a result, the assembly doesn't have to work at filling the church with sound. It is already done for them.

The primary choir is the assembly and they need to hear each other first. The music ministry acts as accompaniment for the assembly's sound. A liturgical choir embellishes the assembly's sound. The liturgical musician is careful not to blast sound into the assembly and replace the assembly's job to fill the church with their voices. If the musicians cannot hear themselves the way the assembly hears them, consider investing in floor monitors to hear right away what the assembly hears.

In some parishes the whole floor of the church is carpeted and the pews are upholstered. Instead of the building carrying sound throughout the room, the cloth on floors and chairs deaden sound. Then leaders have to depend entirely on a sound system to carry the sound in the room. In these settings, there is a fine line between too loud and just right for supporting the assembly. Under all circumstances, resist the temptation to turn up the sound system to the level of a concert group. The group should be heard "live" with only the song leader's instructions amplified. The loudest group should be the assembly.

62.	Our guitar player wrote lots of music for Mass. She put together a hymn book of the words to all the songs she wrote, but why does the liturgy director say we can't use only her songs at Mass?

It's nice that your guitar player is writing music. Such music certainly can be added to seasonal planning so that some of it might be incorporated. However, a steady "diet" of only one composer at any Mass does a disservice to the assembly.

Catholics are members of a church that reaches beyond boundaries. We celebrate our unity in diversity. We sing music from various countries of the world. In this country, some hymns, songs, and acclamations are familiar to other Catholics in the nation. Singing music we have in common with other Catholics helps us to maintain the tension between the local church and the church in the nation and in the world.

No song roster should become so "parochial" as to limit the singing assembly to one composer's music.

63.	*Why can't our folk ensemble use popular songs we hear on the radio or on the Gospel rock station during the Mass?*

The music we sing at Mass contains texts from the liturgy and from the Bible. Our music focuses our attention on the rites we celebrate or on the biblical texts we proclaim.

Some music from the radio might be meditations on Scripture stories or meditations on human relationships (which might seem appropriate at a wedding). Songs like these are appropriate at receptions or parties; however, in the Mass, our song needs to embellish the Scripture of the day or the Mass texts.

64. *Why do the words of our hymns or songs have to be based on Scripture or on the Mass texts?*

The music we sing in the Mass enables us to express our faith as Catholics. We must be sensitive to the theology expressed in the text so that what we sing is Catholic theology. We need to judge whether the music supports a particular rite and the ritual flow of the Mass. We need to discern the way Scripture was interpreted by the composer because Catholics are not fundamentalists. The music we sing primarily expresses our communal faith in the paschal mystery. As a result, a devout solo with "Jesus and me" spirituality may not have a place within a community of believers working to sing in unity in order to express their common faith in the Trinity.

65. *As a choir member, how can I learn more about how to read music?*

In order to learn how to read music to sing, you need to know how to move from one note to the next, how long to hold each note, and how long to hold a particular rest.

Sometimes we liturgical choir directors get so in the habit of rehearsing weekly and seasonal music that we overlook spending time on building choir members' musical skills. Talk with your director about spending ten to fifteen minutes of rehearsal on music skills each time.

Learning how to read music comes with practice. During a rehearsal, the director can choose a hymn or acclamation the group never sang before. Use a syllable in place of the words and sing straight through without stopping (with very little organ or piano to guide you.) Try it with the full accompaniment and with a pencil, mark the places that were difficult for you. After the second time through, stop and identify the difficult places. Did the rhythm cause the problem or the skip from one note to the next? Ask for guidance on your problem place. Then, with the organ or piano playing melody on octaves, sing the whole hymn one more time. Then, put it away and move on to the next piece to rehearse. Adults learn well with a bit of pressure with a short but potent exercise. The choir members may not be the best at it for a while but a director should persist. Each time, use a different and unknown hymn. The goal is to read something new each week.

Also, ask the director to take a few minutes each rehearsal to get the group to sing a C-major scale and name each note. The director can have fun after a while, pointing to different notes out of order for the group to sing and name.

On your own, you can get a basic how-to book from the library that will name each note of the scale. Make a picture for yourself with staff lines and notes of the C-major scale and tape it to your bathroom mirror. Every morning, read and say the name of the note. Then move to sing and say the notes. Gradually, this experience will strengthen your sight-reading and help you to read other music.

66. *We feel pressure to learn a new piece of music each week. How can we overcome this pressure?*

If you are using the weekly psalm assigned in the lectionary and if your group has to have a new piece each week, you are indeed under a lot of pressure. Consider using the option of the seasonal psalm so the musicians and the assembly can memorize the psalm over time and savor each word. That will also take some pressure off the group to present a new and musically appealing psalm setting each week.

The choir or ensemble member, cantor, and director can also benefit from a five-year plan for group music and assembly music. To strengthen the participation of everyone concerned, the liturgical music leader can convene all leaders to sketch one plan for the whole parish. The goal is to take the pressure off, strengthen the group sound, and help everyone (including the assembly) to sing with confidence.

Outline the assembly's repertoire for a period of five years. Decide in advance which songs, hymns, and acclamations will be used in the parish per season.

For example, during the Christmas season, which is about three weeks long, decide which six hymns or songs the assembly will sing and which set of eucharistic prayer acclamations (Holy, memorial acclamation, Amen) the parish will do for the next five years. When that is set, each group leader (folk ensemble or choir) can plan eight pieces of music that will be used and repeated each Christmas season for five years. Then, when the season comes up, the group can review and embellish hymns and songs they already know instead of starting from scratch each year.

Plan ahead for each season. As a result, you can practice next season's music six weeks in advance. It is okay to repeat music that promotes a singing assembly!

When the fifth year arrives, evaluate the repertoire. Cut out music that isn't working and insert other music you have reviewed and put on hold during the five-year time period. If you introduce only one new piece per season, that will be plenty.

In the meantime, you will have more time to get to know good music better (and some by heart), and you will be able to give some of the rehearsal time to music and group vocal lessons. This investment in your group can help the musicians grow instead of fall into weekly panic.

Questions From Pastors And Pastoral Leaders

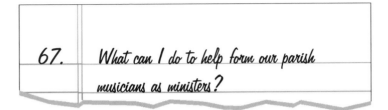

67. *What can I do to help form our parish musicians as ministers?*

As a resource person and leader, you can plan with the liturgy committee chairperson to regularly include a study of *Music in Catholic Worship, Liturgical Music Today,* and the introduction of *Environment and Art in Catholic Worship.* The music leaders, choir director, and cantors should be on this committee. Each time they meet, the group can study these documents, which outline the value for active participation in the liturgy.

Help the leaders to be sensitive to the language they use as they lead. For example, refer to the people in church not as an audience but as an assembly. Talk about the choir as a music ministry group or liturgical choir. Talk less about the choir's performances and more about the way the choir ministers with liturgical music and leads the assembly to sing.

Help the leaders to use seasonal psalms with the assembly so the choir can get the primary choir (the assembly) to sing the melody by heart. Then, the choir can embellish the assembly's song with descants, rounds, and three- or four-part harmony.

Invite the leaders to plan a retreat for all parish musicians where you could function as the spiritual guide and the leaders could teach the group how to think more like ministers of God's word and sacrament through song. Time to retreat away and focus on formation, language, and practice will deeply affect the way parish musicians minister.

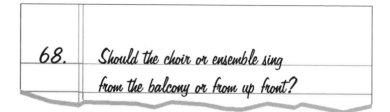

68. *Should the choir or ensemble sing from the balcony or from up front?*

The choir or ensemble is a part of the assembly. As Catholics renovate churches or build new spaces, they build spaces especially designed for musicians within view of the assembly.

> In relation to the design of each church, the *schola cantorum* should be so placed that its character as a part of the assembly of the faithful that has a special function stands out clearly. The location should also assist the choir's liturgical ministry and readily allow each member complete, that is, sacramental participation in the Mass (see *Musicum Sacrum* 23) (GIRM 274).

> The musician belongs first of all to the assembly; he or she is a worshiper above all (LMT 64).

> Benches or chairs for…the ministry of music…should be so constructed and arranged that they have the advantages…[of] congregational seating [a seating pattern and furniture that do not constrict people, but encourage them to move about when it is appropriate (68)] and also that they are clearly part of the assembly (GIRM 274) (EACW 69).

69. *We don't have hymnals. Is it legal to print just the words of songs for the assembly?*

If your parish does not have a hymnal but makes copies of the lyrics of songs, you still must secure permission to print the words. You pay a fee for the right to use the copyrighted music and, in justice, pay the artist for the work produced. You may not be printing the melody line, but you are using it.

You should also consider the cost of paper per year plus the cost of personnel to print the words and run copies. Compare that annual cost over a five-year period in comparison to a one-time purchased hymnal.

Consider the consequences of supplying words only for the assembly. When an assembly has no notation to refer to, they lose access to the visual aid for singing. Their total dependance for learning the melody is on the cantor or choir and we, as leaders, miss the opportunity to help the singers to become musically literate. This doesn't mean that they should stay glued to the hymnal during all parts of the liturgy because I believe certain acclamations and the communion processional music should be sung by heart. However, hymnals allow anyone in the assembly to hospitably provide a copy for strangers and guests who come to join the parish in the liturgy. Even if the strangers or guests don't know the song, the notation can help them participate.

If only words are printed, the assembly loses access to its liturgical repertoire list. Only the music director has a record of what the people have sung. Hymnals list their basic and seasonal repertoire, which can help the baptized when they plan weddings, funerals, and other small group prayer settings.

We should work to assist all ministers in active participation in the liturgy.

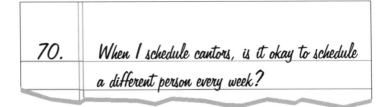

70. *When I schedule cantors, is it okay to schedule a different person every week?*

This way of scheduling can work only if each cantor works from the same repertoire list for the assembly and approaches the ministry with the whole community and its liturgy in mind. If each cantor does not have a parish-wide view of worship music, then communal ownership for the liturgy breaks down. Every cantor should practice humility and submit to the communal plan for liturgical music.

The best situation is that the same cantor remain for four to six weeks at a time so she or he can grow to know the assembly and what will enable their active participation as they sing the liturgy.

The assembly does well when they have built a relationship over time with the cantor. When the assembly is familiar with the cantor, they trust what the leaders ask of them. In turn, you will hear strength and confidence in the song of the assembly.

71. *When the cantor is out of town, why can't we skip having music at Mass that day?*

The normal way we celebrate the liturgy is by singing it. Singing unites the assembly in one voice. The goal is to unite all people in the liturgy. We are active participants who sing, respond, process, and fully, consciously participate.

If the parish has only one or two cantors, the cantors have a responsibility to train more cantors so that this situation does not occur. The assembly must not be cut short of its right to conscious, full, and active participation in the liturgy every time it celebrates it.

72.	*The people are complaining that our cantor sounds like an opera singer and sings too high. What can I do?*

Consider the music the person is singing. Most liturgical music is written so that the highest note is D, nine notes above middle C—a common range for all voices. Even if the higher D is used, most liturgical music does not linger on it but moves up to it and down from it quickly. The assembly handles a range from A, below middle C, to D, nine notes above middle C, with ease.

It is possible to have a man with a bass voice and a woman with a soprano voice sing this range with comfort. What is different between the two is the color of their voices. Sometimes, because a woman's voice may sound light (to the untrained ear, "high"), a person might decide that her voice is "high and operatic-like" and then report that the man's bass voice is easier to hear. Yet, they may be singing in the same range. As leaders, we need to teach our assemblies how to support and include the gifts of all our community artists.

One could discuss other factors with the music director. Do the cantors need a refresher course on the importance of diction? If the cantor is also functioning as a song leader, is the person clear that he or she should not sing the whole hymn, song, or acclamation into the microphone? A cantor supports the assembly as they begin to sing and then backs away from the microphone to blend in with the assembly, who fill the church with sound.

73.	*Sometimes the music director chooses music I consider inappropriate. How can I give feedback in a helpful manner?*

Giving feedback to colleagues is often difficult. Every minister likes to consider himself or herself a capable leader. When we are talking about a person's art form, such as music, we are dealing with an intimate gift.

For example, if you are a homilist, that is your art form. Imagine someone telling you that the topic you chose for a homily may be inappropriate. Imagine the words the person would use. Play it out in your mind and monitor your own reaction. Invite a person or two in the assembly to actually do this over a period of four Sundays. After you have the experience, you will have more information on how to give feedback to the musician.

Next, outline what you consider inappropriate music. Back up your position with the documents *The Constitution on the Sacred Liturgy, Music in Catholic Worship,* and *Liturgical Music Today.* (If you are unable to do this, it may be necessary to reflect on your position further. Is it the music or another issue that affects your judgment?) After you've completed that step in your preparation, be ready to approach the conversation as a teacher. Don't expect to be understood the first time but plant the mustard seed and back off for a while. It is best not to expect to have the situation changed after one meeting on the topic. Be prepared to give the musician some time to read the passages you studied from the documents on his or her own time. Give him or her time to think about it and practice implementing it.

Feedback sessions often fail when a person expects the other to understand immediately and change immediately. Take time to nurture growth.

74. *We have a "guitar Mass," an "organ and choir Mass," and a "piano Mass." How can we celebrate our parish unity with three different kinds of music?*

The people at every Mass in a parish should sing from one roster of music from which each group plays. Parish unity is clear to parishioners when they can go from one Mass time to the next and know the music because it is sung at all Masses.

The united roster of music should include acclamations that can be played on an organ, a piano, or a guitar. Even a simple hymn usually played on an organ, such as "Praise to the Lord," can be done on piano and guitar or piano alone. A flexible liturgical organist with access to a piano can use improvisational skills to play a song with melody and guitar symbols. Every roster of music should include some music typically played either on organ or on guitar. Each music ministry at each Mass should be capable and flexible to play the same roster of music. As a result, each group can minister with hymns, acclamations, songs and chants written for organ, piano, or guitar. Each group can also sing three- or four-part choral music. The director of each group takes time to teach group or choir members some basic sight-reading skills at the beginning of each rehearsal.

Even in parishes where there is a diversity of cultures, parishioners can still celebrate with a unified roster of music. If the Mass is celebrated in the primary language of recent immigrants, it would be important to translate some of their songs and hymns into the other languages of the parish so that at each Mass time the assembly is singing the melody of another cultural group but in their primary language.

A unified roster is essential for the strength of a parish. Additionally, liturgical musicians must continue to grow musically so they can be flexible and celebrate unity in diversity.

75. *How do we determine what is good music for children's liturgies?*

Everything in the liturgy is ultimately a vehicle of faith. In our recent past, music was written specifically for young children to use in the liturgy. Simple music with simple texts is short-lived in the life of the Catholic and very seldom, if ever, finds its way into the parish repertoire for Sunday. Put in another way, music used at the beginning of their life-long formation as Catholics is used for two or three years only. As children grow older, they can claim little from those first years as young Catholics. This sets up a weak foundation for their life-long role as singers of the liturgy.

Children deserve to learn the music for the liturgy that they will sing for the rest of their lives. When they enter the church for a school liturgy, why not hear the organist play Bach's "Prelude in G minor" or the junior high choir sing the soprano and alto line of "Comfort, Comfort Ye My People" with a hand drum, triangle, and guitar? Children love to imitate adults. They can handle the psalms the church sings on Sunday. Children take pride in learning and mastering a few well-written pieces rather than stumbling through ill-prepared, unsatisfying tunes which they won't hear when they return again on Sunday.

When we choose liturgical music for children, we need to think about giving them food for their journey in the life of faith. Which music prepares the child for a life-long vocation to sing the liturgy? Which song, hymn, psalm or acclamation will the child still be singing and cherishing when he or she is old?

We bring our children to the liturgy to be formed by it. The Liturgy of the Word instills in us and in the children the true

Christian spirit, and our actions in the Liturgy of the Eucharist are our responses in faith to God's word. As we grow older, we become aware of the way the Word and Eucharist work together to convert us more deeply every year to God's way of living. Converted to God's way, we go into the world to make the kingdom visible. This is what we expect from the liturgy for our children. Each child learns how to participate actively in the liturgy over a series of years. The main ministry, that of being an active member of the assembly, is the most important ministry in the parish a child can learn. Through this ministry, a child learns how to be the presence of Christ in the world. We know that good liturgy forms Catholics. As the bishops have so succinctly put it, "Good celebrations foster and nourish faith. Poor celebrations may weaken and destroy it" (*Music in Catholic Worship* 6).

---

76. *Why can't our university choir sing choir songs during Mass?*

Although the university choir (or any secular performance group) may know some Catholic motets or settings of psalms, their mission is very different from a liturgical choir's. Their mission is to perform music of various epochs in music history with as much attention as possible to the performance practices of the time. The role they take is that of performer, and the audience is a passive listener.

A liturgical choir's mission is different. Their primary focus or mission is to support and encourage the active participation of the primary choir, the assembly. The music they prepare is music that is focused on the liturgy. Music does not stand on its own in our liturgy. Music for the Mass is focused on the assembly, who sing the texts of the liturgy and of Scripture. Our document *Liturgical Music Today* says:

> The church musician is first a disciple and then a minister.
> The musician belongs first of all to the assembly; he or she
> is a worshiper above all. Like any member of the assembly,
> the pastoral musician needs to be a believer, needs to
> experience conversion, needs to hear the Gospel and so
> proclaim the praise of God. Thus, the pastoral musician is
> not merely an employee or volunteer. He or she is a
> minister, someone who shares faith, serves the community,
> and expresses the love of God and neighbor through
> music (64).

Unless the university choir can sing the liturgy, support and encourage the song of the assembly, and express their faith, they should not assume a role of music ministry at the liturgy. If they sing one or two songs during the Mass in harmony with their mission—to perform—then we are not doing justice to our continued mission. Instead we deform attitudes about the purpose of music groups in the liturgy.

A university choir or any choir from an educational institution that will not function as a liturgical choir in the liturgy should be invited to sing a concert after the liturgy is over or at a later time.

77.	Our renovation committee wants to replace our antique electric organ and our spinet piano with a grand piano. Is this appropriate? Do we need an organ anymore?

A number of factors should be considered: the size of the church room, the acoustics (is carpet deadening sound?), the number of people who gather at each liturgy, the many kinds of music done in the liturgy, the size and placement of the choir, and the budget and potential fund raising.

It is a good idea to replace a spinet piano (smallest size) with a grand piano. It is also a good idea to replace the organ. If your electric organ is an antique, it might be powered by dated materials that no longer exist (for example, electronic vacuum tubes instead of transistors and computer parts).

The committee should go to other Catholic and Protestant churches to listen to pipe organs during their services. These organs are custom built to suit the size and acoustic needs of the church building. After the committee visits at least three churches with pipe organs, they are better equipped to discern the kinds of organs to investigate.

Even if you have no organist at the present time, the parish should responsibly plan for the future, recruit a musician in their midst to support by training him or her to be the parish organist, and keep all options open for the many kinds of music the liturgy deserves. I would not limit the song of the assembly by putting in only a piano.

After the Second Vatican Council, the role of the organ changed. The assembly began to sing. The organ skills of most Catholic organists at the time were not suited for assembly singing. Organists were told that they sounded "muddy" or that their hymn playing was poor. Yet, they were using a style they had learned to accompany a pre-Vatican II liturgy full of lyrical Gregorian chant.

The size of the singing assembly required Catholic organists to explore and study other ways to accompany a much larger group of singers than a choir of a chosen few. Wisely, some organists turned to our Christian brothers and sisters and adopted hymn-playing skills from their four-hundred-year experience of accompanying a singing assembly. These skills helped Catholic organists to play clearly. An organist plays the notes of the melody clearly by detaching each note. (The previous style required that the organist connect each note.) Catholic organists combined these skills to effectively accompany a singing assembly.

When a well-trained organist plays, the organ can produce the sound of a great symphony and support the song of many singers. It can also produce a small sound when needed. Before the committee rules out an organ, it should take time to visit a church with a fine organ and a fine organist to explore these ideas further.

Renovation committees should examine the music needs of the sung liturgy and provide the instruments the assembly needs. Take time to talk with professional liturgical organists and pianists.

---

78. Why is it bad to carpet the church floor?

Carpet is not the best material for the floors of churches. Overlooking the effects of spilled wax or charcoal, water marks, sparks from candles, or soiled high-traffic areas, carpet inhibits a singing assembly.

In a carpeted church, the scope of sound around each singer is small. The carpet absorbs sound as soon as it is made. The singer feels like he or she is singing alone. Few Catholics feel the confidence to sing alone and when they think they are alone, they tend to stop. They complain that they "can't hear anyone."

The way communities attempt to remedy this problem is to turn up the sound system until the assembly has sound blasted at them. The result is that the people eventually stop singing because the sound system allows the cantor or choir to fill the building with sound. Filling the church with song (singing) is the "work" of the people, but in this scenario, electronic sound is filling the church, giving the assembly the "option" to join the "church full of sound" already made (by a few—the choir or cantor plus accompanying instruments) electronically. Thoughtful pastoral leaders resist this because it affects the active participation of the baptized in the liturgy.

Hard-surfaced floors under the assembly, the choir, and the altar or ambo area reflect sound and make it easier for each person to sing. Once a person sings, the sound dances on the hard surface and mixes with the sounds of other singers. An inexperienced singer feels supported and encouraged to sing because of the live sound around him or her. There is less need for sound systems to do the work of the natural sound of many voices singing in unity (active participation).

Any surface with cloth and foam will do the same for the singing assembly as carpet on the floor. It will absorb sound immediately. Observe that when choirs sing in concert halls, for example, they do not sit on chairs of any kind.

Now, our assemblies are not engaged in a concert but each assembly is the primary choir. We need to do everything we can to support their efforts in making a beautiful sound together and not deter their efforts with sound absorbers.

Paying
Liturgical
Music
Directors

79.	*Why do we have to pay someone to do music for Mass? Why can't we use volunteers?*

Because our liturgy is a sung liturgy, it is our responsibility to provide music consistently at every Mass every week. Because we express and deepen our faith by actively participating in the liturgy, we need to make certain that the music leader is present at each liturgy, is trained, and is aware of the important influence music ministry has in the lives of believers.

Sometimes it is possible to invite a volunteer to this ministry. Conscientious volunteers are there each week and arrange substitutes when they are absent; however, simply because a person volunteers to be the music leader and can be there each week does not necessarily qualify the person for the ministry. The parish liturgy team or committee should invite the volunteer to audition for the position in order to demonstrate musical skills. This audition should occur in front of the committee and (if the group considers the volunteer a possible candidate for the position) at one liturgy. In this way, the group can examine the volunteer's knowledge of liturgy and liturgical music.

Unskilled (instrumentally or vocally) or uncertain musicians call attention to themselves because of their inabilities and interrupt the flow of the liturgy. A well-trained musician, on the other hand, is able to do music with ease and weave the music in the liturgy. He or she directs the assembly's attention to singing the liturgy.

If the volunteer is judged capable, the liturgy team or committee should consider a weekly stipend for the person anyway. It is an act of justice to recognize one who plays an instrument well and invests time, talent, and treasure into developing that ability. Paying a stipend ensures that the person will have an official relationship with the parish team (or pastor) and that he or she can be supervised by a qualified person. Even volunteers should have a job description, a designated supervisor, and an annual review. A review creates a built-in time to renew commitments so that one is not assumed into a ministry for life. The parish also has a right to expect Christian behavior, effective leadership, and quality ministry from the person.

On the other hand, hiring a music director can ensure consistent weekly music by writing this expectation into the job description. Again, a candidate for the position should be auditioned and questioned about his or her knowledge of liturgy and liturgical music. More can be expected of a person the parish plans to hire for the position. A music director can supervise other volunteers, teach them how to improve their skills, and build up the parish music ministry.

In either case, the spiritual health of the parish community is at stake. Since ours is a sung liturgy, each parish needs a faithful and qualified leader of liturgical music.

80. What does a liturgical music director do?

The liturgical music director shares faith. He or she builds relationships with parishioners so he or she knows who the choir must motivate and lead in the singing of the liturgy. He or she recruits faith-filled parishioners for the choir, convenes the choir, and directs it. This involves invitations in person or over the phone.

Concerned always about the singing assembly, the liturgical music director sees to it that the assembly has a hymnal that makes the parish liturgy repertoire of music accessible to each person. The director should be in charge of maintaining the supply of hymnals so that each copy will reflect the dignity of the prayer and the work at hand.

This person is a leader with parish committee groups, too, working with the parish staff and liturgy committee to promote the mission of the universal church and the local parish.

There should be weekly rehearsals with the choir (or choirs) for musical, catechetical, and spiritual formation. The director should be musically flexible to lead a mixed choir and a folk ensemble and/or a combination of the two.

The director leads a well-organized rehearsal, which should include prayer, fun, accurate catechetical instruction when it applies, musical instruction (choir members should learn to read music over the course of a year), and group voice lessons. Effective rehearsals can educate and catechize members on all aspects of music, liturgical music-making, liturgy in general, and evangelization. The director needs time and space to plan and to prepare the musical score. He or she prepares the scores, highlighting difficult passages or transitions, challenging harmonization, and balance issues for the choir prior to rehearsal.

Because the liturgical musician knows the liturgical year and the lectionary, he or she chooses music appropriate to the Scripture and season. He or she chooses music for the assembly and music for the choir groups.

This is not a complete job description, but it may give you a basic outline from which to work.

81.	*Our parish liturgy committee recommends that the parish hire a full-time music director. What benefit is there in hiring a director?*

Your parish liturgy committee is probably familiar with the *Constitution on the Sacred Liturgy*, which calls for trained musicians for the liturgy. A trained musician is an asset to the singing assembly. A faith-filled Catholic person trained in liturgical music can guide parish music leaders toward quality liturgical music in the parish. The person can convene parish musicians and develop an overall liturgical music program for the parish liturgies. He or she can organize in-service gatherings to strengthen music skills and knowledge of the liturgy.

We must strive toward quality liturgical music. We find in *Music in Catholic Worship*, the statement from our American bishops, that good liturgy strengthens faith and that poor liturgies may weaken or destroy faith. The liturgy must be good so that the faith of all people will be strengthened.

Music is an integral part of the liturgy. Intimately bound to the rite, it enables the expression of our faith. It requires a response from us, and when it is powerful, we respond emotionally and spiritually.

In the liturgy, God's word is creative. When we celebrate the Liturgy of the Word in song and proclamation, God creates faith in us. In the Liturgy of the Eucharist, we respond and acclaim our faith by our action. We share the Body and Blood of Christ and then go forth to be the Body of Christ in the world, transforming the world. Good liturgical music is essential for this experience in liturgy.

If the music is bad, it will suffocate the power of the liturgy. Many of us have been to liturgies in which the music was weak or done incorrectly. We try to follow well-meaning leaders who have difficulty singing melodies or playing instruments correctly. In these settings, music is no longer a servant to the liturgy because our attention is called to the struggling person and his or her fractured attempts to inspire and lead the singing assembly. We go from those liturgies talking about the distraction—the music leader's level of skill—instead of pondering the Word of God and the call to be the Body of Christ in the world.

When your parish hires a music coordinator or director, the volunteers do not retire. A trained music director enables the volunteers to grow stronger and more capable. The trained person leads but also teaches others how to lead capably so that all will focus without distraction on our celebration of word and sacrament. He or she is like an on-site "coach" for volunteer liturgical musicians. She or he can also help volunteers to shape a parish-wide five-year repertoire list for the assembly based on the musical, liturgical and pastoral judgment.

A salaried music coordinator (or director) enters into an agreement that she or he is accountable to the parish. The parish assigns a supervisor and the musician understands that his or her time and talent belong to the parish community.

The musician coordinates the time and talent of parish volunteers and supervises their ministry. She or he is responsible for helping to build strong liturgies, enabling active participation of the assembly, and building the quality and accountability of a parish music ministry.

The goal of the liturgy is to celebrate the presence of Christ in word and sacrament so the assembly can go forth to evangelize and transform the world. We need to do all we can to ensure the experience of liturgy is clear and well communicated.

82. *How do we interview candidates for the position of director of liturgical music?*

If you are at the point of interviewing, you have completed the initial steps. You have outlined the parish's need for a music director. You have written the job description from your outline. You have advertised in the parish bulletin, in diocesan networks, through campus job-posting centers, with friends, and on-line. Talk with inquirers over the phone after you receive their resumes to discern which individuals you will invite for an interview. You may save time if, for example, the inquirer cannot manage the range of pay you are offering or if the conversation reveals the person is better skilled in another area.

When you invite the person to interview, outline for him or her how to prepare for the interview. For example, you will want him or her to play a hymn, an acclamation, and a prelude piece on the organ (or piano, depending on which instrument you have in the parish). You will want to witness the way the person would lead a psalm and a hymn so you can get an idea of his or her leadership style and vocal production. If the person comes from a parish experience, ask to see copies of the music rosters he or she planned for liturgical seasons such as Advent, Easter (Easter to Pentecost), and winter Ordinary Time. The person could provide copies of rehearsal outlines with choirs. All this information will give you insight into the person's music skills and organization skills needed for effective leadership.

The interview team should be no larger than four or five people. The team can consist of a member of the assembly, a member of the parish music ministry, the pastor, and a lay staff person. Try to arrange to have at least two people to interview.

About thirty minutes before the first interview, the team should gather together to focus their task. They might review the questions they as a team will ask. The team should have a list of about eight questions they agree will most effectively gather information about the person's liturgical knowledge, musical knowledge, and willingness to be supervised and to work with a staff. These eight questions should be agreed upon by the team before the interviews and a copy of the eight questions given to each team member.

At the interview, welcome the inquirer into a comfortable room and make introductions with the team members. It is a good idea to ask the inquirer to tell the group about him- or herself. During the interview, keep the inquirer talking. Ask him or her to name some acclamations that are a part of the national repertoire for Catholic churches. Ask the person to explain how he or she plans and schedules music so the assembly can sing. Ask the person to describe the liturgical year, the names of each season, and the story told. Ask the person to name at least one hymn or song that depicts a particular season. Members of the team might ask questions but mostly listen—this is not a time to tell parish stories to the inquirer.

Following the questions and discussion, the interview might move to the worship space where the candidate can perform on organ, piano, guitar, and voice. Ask the person to present a psalm to the group the way he or she would introduce it to the assembly and the way he or she would cantor the text. Invite the candidate to teach the interview group a basic lesson in sight-reading geared for cantors and choir members. Every director of liturgical music should see him- or herself as a teacher of the liturgy and a teacher of music. The person should teach the interviewing group a choral piece in three- or four-part harmony so you can get an idea of how the person rehearses a choir. Invite the person to play a hymn on the piano or organ and lead the interview group in a full hymn. If the person also knows the guitar, ask him or her to lead the interview group in a hymn or song using the guitar to support harmony and rhythm.

Team members should take notes to remember one candidate's qualifications from the others'.

After each interview, the team should spend ten minutes summarizing the strengths and weaknesses observed before moving on to the next person. Interview all inquirers before announcing your preference or decision to the team.

When the team makes its choice, a letter should go out to all other inquirers to thank them for applying and to announce that the team made its choice. A team member might call the chosen musician to announce the choice, but a letter from the pastor should follow to affirm this and to outline the terms such as salary, hours per week, benefits, and starting date.

When the new person arrives for the first day of work, someone should be on hand to show the musician his or her office space and music ministry space and to present keys to the facilities.

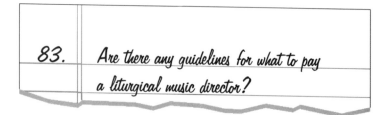

83. *Are there any guidelines for what to pay a liturgical music director?*

Y es. Check the American Guild of Organists (see their address and e-mail address below), The Association of Lutheran Church Musicians, your diocesan worship office or neighboring diocesan office, and other liturgical musicians in your area. There is also a website available to calculate a salary should you ask a person to move from one major city to another and wish to know how much more they might need to earn in order to maintain their present standard of living (http://www.homefair.com/homefair/cmr/salcalc.html).

Remember that a liturgical music director is responsible for the spiritual formation of each person in your parish. It is worth your time to not only interview well and check references but also, once the committee has made the choice, to pay the person a just salary.

The American Guild of Organists
Councillor for Professional Concerns
Eileen Guenther, DMA
Foundry United Methodist Church
1500 16th Street NW
Washington, DC 20036
202-332-4010
202-332-4035 (FAX)
http://www.agohq.org/profession/

The Association of Lutheran Church Musicians
ALCM Administrator, PO Box 1873,
Valparaiso, IN 46384; 219-548-9004

Questions From The Assembly

---

84. *Who chooses the music for Sunday Mass —
the organist, Father, the choir director?*

This is an easy question to answer if there is only one Mass on Sunday and a small staff of musicians. In that case, the presider, the choir director, and the organist can work together and shape the whole liturgy based on the Scripture for a particular Sunday. Although the presider may not be involved in choosing music specifically, his point of view is important in relationship to the question, "How well is the assembly singing the liturgy?"

If there are many Mass times and the music director functions at every Mass every weekend, that person might choose the music. But if that person isn't participating at Mass every week and the organist or accompanist for the assembly is, then the organist should be the primary planner of the assembly's song. The person with the most contact with the assembly can focus on how well the assembly is singing the choice of music.

This is a more difficult question to address when there are multiple Masses in one parish on a Sunday and there is no one music director hired to choose music for the whole parish. If there are different music leaders at each Mass time, it is the responsibility of the pastor to convene the leaders and assemble a parish-wide list of acclamations, hymns, and songs that each leader uses. This is essential so that a parishioner can feel at home at any Mass time and feel enabled to actively participate with a unified repertoire of music. Where there is a bilingual or trilingual assembly with two or more liturgies celebrated in different languages, it is important to convene the leaders of the different language groups and choose music that is bilingual and that can be interchangeably used at various liturgy times. When no bilingual music exists, it takes the effort of music leaders to try, for example, a musical setting of a psalm or acclamation in two languages and make translations where possible. At least the melodies can unify the assemblies though the language might be different.

Using the same or similar music for all Mass times is the goal.

85. *Why do we have to learn so much new music?*

The answer is, we don't. If you are learning a new hymn or a new Holy every week, you have the responsibility to talk with the music leadership and the presider. Obviously, there is a problem to solve. Be part of the solution. Ask to be a member of the music planning group or the liturgy committee. Let both the presider and music leaders know up front that you would like to explore ways to strengthen the singing assembly with the use of repetition.

Next, be prepared to identify some acclamations, songs, and hymns you feel very comfortable singing. Try not to work in isolation. Seek out your neighbors in the assembly and ask what their favorites are.

Finally, be prepared to learn new things, too. This is a worthy question and a worthy task. The Gospel values will shine because of the way the project is approached and the way people are honored as the solution comes about.

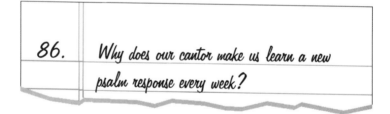

86. *Why does our cantor make us learn a new psalm response every week?*

When the music director or cantor plans a season or a series of weeks in Ordinary Time, he or she has two options: 1) to locate musical settings for the psalm listed in the lectionary each week, or 2) to plan a seasonal psalm, in which case the cantor leads the assembly in one of the psalms of the season for the duration of the season.

When the music director decides to use the psalm assigned for each Sunday, the musical setting of the psalm response the assembly sings will be different each week. Each psalm text requires its own melody. As a result, you learn a new psalm response melody every Sunday.

When seasonal psalms are used, the assembly sings the same refrain, for example, during the six Sundays of Lent.

Because you are learning a new psalm response every week, your leader is using the psalm for the day.

87.	*When our choir sings, we like them so much we just listen to them. If we like the choir, why can't we just listen?*

People in the assembly sometimes expect that the choir in worship follows the entertainment model as seen in concert halls or on television. However, if the assembly only listens to the choir, they become an audience who look at, listen to, and judge the group; they are consumers instead of worshipers.

Everything the choir is and does should make it clear to the assembly that the choir is not an entertaining or concert group. The music they sing should enable the baptized to sing the liturgy.

The choir should be placed within the assembly so it is clear that they are members of the assembly. Their ministerial-leadership role requires that the assembly see the choir and the choir see the assembly. They should avoid any setting resembling a stage. As a result, the assembly will focus on what is going on in the liturgy as opposed to focusing on the musicians and their music.

Some musicians find it difficult to focus liturgical music on the assembly, but liturgical music engages people in a dialogue. When it is done well, the assembly remembers the whole experience of the liturgy more than they remember a particular piece of music or a particular musician. We know that a person needs a healthy ego to be able to make music in public or preside at a liturgy or proclaim the Scripture. The practice of humility in these ministries means that the person offers his or her talents to the whole experience so that the experience of the liturgy will convert hearts. The goal is not to do music so well that people will compliment "me" or "my choir." The goal is to be a part of an assembly of people who are offering various talents to the best of their ability so that people will talk about Jesus and the wonders of his life and teaching.

The assembly has a right and duty to experience the whole liturgy and to participate in it actively. Our work is to be a part of a pool of ministries who express faith by singing the liturgy, which will engage and inspire all people to the mission of Jesus Christ.

88. Can't we use a Marian hymn at every Mass?

Marian hymns or songs are appropriately chosen for Marian feasts or particular seasonal celebrations such as the Fourth Sunday of Advent. The text of a hymn or song is chosen to illuminate the Gospel or other Scripture of the day. A text might be chosen also to illuminate the ritual at a particular time in the liturgy such as the communion procession.

To choose a hymn or song just because it is a Marian text without regard to the Scripture of the day or the season is inappropriate.

> The first place to look for guidance in the use and choice of music is the rite itself. Often the rubrics contained in the approved liturgical books will indicate the place for song, and will also prescribe or suggest an appropriate text to be set musically (LMT 8).

In another place, the document reminds us that

> sacramental celebrations are significant moments in an individual's life, but just as importantly they are constitutive events of the community's life in Christ. The music selected must express the prayer of those who

celebrate, while at the same time guarding against the imposition of private meanings on public rites. Individual preference is not, of itself, a sufficient principle for the choice of music in the liturgy (12).

The liturgical musicians who choose music for the assembly practice a healthy sense of humility every time they choose music with the guidelines above. It is a selfless act focused on the spiritual formation and conversion of an assembly of Catholics throughout the liturgical year.

As liturgical musicians choose music, they also use the musical-liturgical-pastoral judgment. Not one of these judgments ever outweighs the other or is considered separately. Rather, all three judgments operate at the same time.

89. Why does my neighbor's parish sing different music than my parish?

Although the Catholic church is a universal church, it teaches "unity in diversity." Within our diverse ways of being in the world, with our varied cultures and ethnic groups, the Catholic liturgy is the same celebration of the Word and Eucharist. Music can be different in various countries and even in different parishes within the same city.

Within the same city, parishes may be using a different music publisher or hymnal as the source for the assembly's song. The Catholic Church in the United States does not have a universal English hymnal or even a national hymnal. (The Church in Canada, however, does have a national hymnal.) This is the basic reason why different Catholic churches in the United States might be singing different music.

90. Do we have to sing at funerals?

Yes. The liturgy in the Catholic Church is sung liturgy. It is our responsibility to make certain that there is music at funerals and that this music is chosen with the same principles used for Sunday liturgy. We must assume the presence of an assembly of people who participate actively in the liturgy. It is true that not all relatives of the deceased will actively participate but other relatives and friends will support them with their responsive prayer and singing. In some parishes, a music leader organizes a choir to sing for the funeral Mass or celebration. Retired people and parents with children at home are important resources for the choir. If the parish music leader or accompanist (organist-pianist) cannot be with the choir for funeral liturgies, he or she can rehearse and prepare the choir in case accompaniment is not available. For these situations, the music leader can choose music that can be sung without accompaniment.

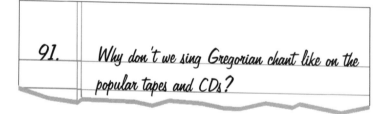

91. Why don't we sing Gregorian chant like on the popular tapes and CDs?

Gregorian chant is beautiful music. It is music that reflects an important time in our church history and music history in general.

In the early church, Gregorian chant was sung by the people in the language of the people. It served the rite. Through the years, professional musicians developed a preferred style of singing the chant, which only choirs could sing. As the church moved into the future, it faced the Reformation and many theological challenges which caused leaders to draw the line between what was Catholic music and what was not Catholic music. Church leaders cautiously defined the Roman Catholic liturgy, its music, and its theology and froze it in time.

Change began in the early 1900s when church leaders noted the need for a pastoral judgment in the liturgical and musical equation. By the 1960s, the church restored the use of the vernacular in the liturgy in favor of active participation in the liturgy through the Second Vatican Council. We recovered the formative dimension of the liturgy in order to instill the true Christian spirit in each person in the assembly.

Because the Second Vatican Council recognized the importance of the vernacular in the liturgy, music in the Catholic liturgy had to change. The church was no longer only European. It had spread all over the world to cultures in Asia, Africa, the Americas, and the Pacific rim peoples. Clearly, the church was not sent to one particular culture or race or nation. Present in these various nations, the church flourished in popular devotions because the melodies, rhythms, instruments, and texts of the host culture were allowed in these non-liturgical celebrations. The people expressed their faith freely in the devotions.

Once the vernacular was again allowed, the power of the language of the people in the experience of liturgical celebration and the catechetical dimension of the liturgy was too powerful to ignore.

In the United States, there was an attempt to use the English with Gregorian chant. However, liturgical musicians quickly discovered that using the vernacular over melody lines developed for the Latin language made the melodies bumpy and jolting. Composers began to write liturgical music suited to the language of each country so that the baptized could sing with grace and dignity.

We still haven't completely actualized the renewal of the liturgy since the Second Vatican Council. There is much more for us to unfold.

In the meantime, today in the United States, it is possible to hear a Latin motet during the prelude to Mass, to sing a gathering song in the primary language of the assembly, to sing the acclamations to the eucharistic prayer bilingually, and to chant the Agnus Dei in Latin to various invocations of Christ during the fraction rite. We have a great prism of ritual music from which to draw.

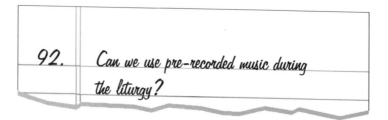

92. *Can we use pre-recorded music during the liturgy?*

Liturgy is an expression of faith for the assembly of believers. Pre-recorded music robs the assembly of their rightful role of singing the liturgy and expressing their faith in song. It should never be used to replace the assembly, organist, other instrumentalists, cantor, or choir.

Whether music is instrumental or not, recorded music lacks the presence of the music-maker, who interacts with the flow of the liturgy, the length of the rite, and the timing of an acclamation in the midst of a spoken prayer or text. Liturgy is a living experience of worship and praise which requires the hearts, minds, and spirits of people involved in the liturgy.

The documents clearly say that recorded music should not be used in the place of the assembly's song. Additionally, it should not be used "in the case of the responsorial psalm after a reading from Scripture or during the optional hymn of praise after communion" (LMT 61).

Liturgy is based on dialogue and relationships between "live" human beings. The ministry of an actively participating assembly is primary and requires the ministry of the musician, the lector, the minister of communion, and the presider to complete the ongoing dialogue. The presider greets the assembly; the assembly greets the presider. The lector proclaims the word; the assembly listens to the proclamation, ponders, and gives thanks. The communion minister holds up the cup and proclaims the presence of Christ, and the baptized proclaim their "Amen." The cantor sings the verses; the assembly responds with the refrain. Ministry in the liturgy involves an intimate relationship between people in which faith is expressed and deepened. When the musician is there in person, the musician can initiate the time when the music begins and respond at the time when the assembly sings acclamations.

We could record the lines of the presider with pauses for the assembly to respond but the ridiculous absence of the presider would kill the spirit and purpose of the liturgy. How can we express faith in our God who initiates a relationship with us and nurtures that relationship through his holy priesthood of believers when we limit a relationship to lines spoken and recorded? We multi-faceted beings need the face, the gestures, the spirit, the touch, the personality, and the text to express the wonder of God. Likewise, using recorded music robs us of the instrumentalist, the cantor, the choir, and the many dimensions of human relationships expressed with the help of liturgical musicians.

---

93. *Protestant churches have prelude music before their services. Is that a good idea for Catholics?*

Yes. The prelude music should start seven to ten minutes before the liturgy. (The organist or pianist or director has carefully timed the prelude and knows how much time to plan for it.) A prelude can consist of an organ prelude, a piano prelude, or the choir or ensemble singing a prepared piece. It is important to note that because we are helping the assembly to move into a community mindset, the prelude should be uplifting, inspiring, or energetic. (It is not a time for music with a secular message. The prelude helps the assembly to focus on the Christian message.)

If your parish has an organist who can play Bach, Vaughn Williams, or Buxtehude, the prelude might consist of a work on the organ during which the musicians and assembly take time to settle their spirits as they process into the church, greet their Christian brothers and sisters, and focus on becoming one in spirit with the community.

If the prelude is done by the choir, ensemble, or cantor, they process into the worship space and take their places after they have warmed up their voices in another room.

94. What ever happened to the silent Mass or low Mass?

When we gather together, we do not gather together to savor community silence. We gather to proclaim the word, to break open the word, to respond to the word in the eucharistic action, to celebrate our unity in the Body and Blood of Jesus, and to be sent into the world to transform it. Liturgy is action. Sacraments are action. "The liturgy is a celebration—not a meditation" (Diess, *Spirit and Song* 105). We are to celebrate every Mass with an actively participating people who sing, respond, gesture, and process. *Music in Catholic Worship* reminds us that

> among the many signs and symbols used by the Church to celebrate its faith, music is of preeminent importance....
> Music should assist the assembled believers to express and share the gift of faith that is within them and to nourish and strengthen their interior commitment of faith (23).

Meditation is what we Catholics do in preparation for the liturgy. We ponder the word of God in our personal prayer and bring the insight of meditation to the liturgy to celebrate it.

There has never been a completely "silent Mass." Even the low Mass of pre-Vatican II days consisted of the priest offering the prayers aloud and the acolyte responding aloud (on our behalf.) In the United States during the 1930s, Father Virgil Michel, OSB, published the *Kyriale* so the Catholic assembly could sing the Mass parts together.

Some Catholics call a Mass without music a "silent Mass." Although some parishes do this, it is not a practice in line with the Second Vatican Council's vision for liturgy. The liturgy is not a passive experience. If anyone joins an assembly and does not sing, respond, gesture, and process but remains passive the whole time, that person's faith is not being expressed. Our faith must be expressed in the signs and symbols of celebration—of which music is one—to remain vibrant. So, it doesn't make sense to have a "quiet Mass" because any leader who allows it risks limiting and suppressing the faith of those who assemble.

The normal Mass of today is one with a priest, a cantor, and a lector, and the people singing the liturgy.

Many Cultures, One Mass

> **95.** *Father and the musicians are making us sing Spanish songs once in a while because some Spanish-speaking families moved into the parish. Why can't the Spanish-speaking people sing English songs with us?*

Attempting to pray and sing the liturgy in a second language is a distracting experience. Try it yourself. Go to a liturgy celebrated only in Spanish and try to pray and sing. The Second Vatican Council recognized that the liturgy can best fill all Catholics with the true Christian spirit and convert their lives if they understand the words of the prayers, responses, and songs. When we pray and sing, we express our faith. By expressing our faith, we strengthen the faith of others and ourselves. When faith is not expressed, it dies.

Historically, when it was not possible to celebrate the liturgy in one's own language, the church relied on devotional prayers for spiritual formation. That is what happened to Catholics when the use of the vernacular language of the people died out and Latin became the one language of the liturgy. Many devotions rose up outside of the eucharistic liturgy because devotions could be celebrated in one's own language.

Some Spanish-speaking Americans are bilingual. If you are part of a dominant English-speaking group in your parish, invite the Spanish-speaking and their bilingual friends to your next liturgy committee meeting. Ask them what it is like to celebrate and sing in English.

96. What is inculturation in the liturgy?

The liturgy is the place the people of God express and strengthen their faith. In each country and culture of the world, the way the people of God do this is unique to each culture. The appearance of the worship space and furnishings, the methods of relationships between people, the language, the music (the shape of melody, use of rhythm, the kinds of instruments, manner of singing), the way people organize the community, their daily dress, methods of teaching and learning—all make up culture. When we talk about inculturation in the liturgy, we need to begin with a view from the universal church. Our expression of inculturation as a universal (catholic) church was heightened when church leaders allowed us to use the language of the people in the liturgy, starting in the early 1960s. Throughout the world, we celebrate word and sacrament with the same Roman Catholic rite (unity) but through various cultures (diversity.) This remarkable experience, unity in our diversity, is an amazing reality. The church dares to practice what our various nations struggle with. With this, the church has the power to bring our practice into the world to transform the world.

Rome has defined inculturation as "an intimate transformation of the authentic cultural values by their integration into Christianity and the implantation of Christianity into different human cultures" (*Roman Liturgy and Inculturation* [January 25, 1994], 4).

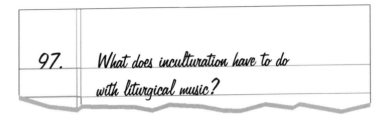

97. *What does inculturation have to do with liturgical music?*

Many believe that inculturation means the assembly sings songs and acclamations in different languages in one liturgy. Others believe it means singing music in the style of one's homeland and one's language. Some extend the opening procession and presentation of gifts procession with people representing various nations present in the assembly and call that experience inculturation. For others, the celebration of devotions with the language and songs of the people is an expression of inculturation. However, inculturation is more than that.

Anscar Chupungco, OSB, who has written books and articles on the subject, says:

> Liturgical inculturation, viewed from the side of the liturgy
> (the side of culture deserves a separate study), may be
> defined as the process of inserting the texts and rites of the
> liturgy into the framework of the local culture. As a result,
> the texts and rites assimilate the people's thought,
> language, values, ritual, symbolic, and artistic pattern
> (*Liturgical Inculturation* 30).

He says that the liturgy is inserted into the culture to "think, speak, and ritualize according to the local cultural pattern. If we settle for anything less than this, the liturgy of the local church will remain at the periphery place of cultural pattern in the process of inculturation" (30).

Inculturation means that there is an interaction between the Christian faith and the culture. Each encompasses elements of the other. Christian faith tends to Christianize some cultural practices as, for example, Advent and Christmas transformed the pagan practices of solstice into the Christian celebration of the coming of the light of Christ. Inculturation, for the Roman Catholic Church, is not a new invention. It has been practiced for centuries.

For example, a missionary walks into a culture not Roman or Italian, a culture other than the culture in which she lives. She must abandon all the structures and assumptions of her home culture. She opens herself to learning the structures and assumptions of the new culture. The first door to this openness is the language of the people. Using the language of the people involves building a relationship with them.

The church recognizes this reality when it says that the first door to inculturation is language. The Bible and the texts of the liturgy need to be translated into the language of the people. However, if these texts are accepted in the new culture, the culture will change and, as a result, the church too will experience some change. The church asserts that change does not mean that portions of the liturgy may be adjusted without the consent of church authorities. It means that the expression of faith within the Catholic liturgy will look and sound and be different in the new culture. The expression of faith will be a unique blend of Catholic spirituality, the paschal mystery, and the spirit and life of the new culture. The liturgy in the new culture will respect "the substantial unity of the Roman rite, the unity of the whole church and the integrity of the faith transmitted to the saints for all time," according to *Instruction: Inculturation and the Roman Liturgy*. This recent Roman document on liturgical inculturation reminds liturgical musicians that "music and singing, which express the soul of people...must be promoted, in the first place...[so they will be] singing the liturgical text, so that the voices of the faithful may be heard in the liturgical actions themselves." It also recognizes that, regarding music, "a text which is sung is more deeply engraved in the memory than when it is read, which means that it is necessary to be demanding about the biblical and liturgical inspiration and the literary quality of texts which are meant to be sung."

Chupungco says that inculturation is more than an external adaptation. "It signifies an interior transformation of authentic cultural values through their integration into Christianity and the rooting of Christianity in various human cultures" (*Liturgical Inculturation* 29). In the process of inculturation, the liturgy and the culture meet and interact, creating a new crossroads for the celebration of the liturgy of that local church.

Inculturation, though, is different from cross-culturation, as we shall see in Question 98.

98. What is meant by cross-cultural music?

We can talk about cross-cultural music by observing the church in the United States. When people of various nations throughout the world move to the United States to live in diverse neighborhoods, we experience a crossing of cultures. In a cross-cultural parish, all cultural assumptions are called into question. The manner of food preparation, of interpersonal relationships, of styles of music, and of determining what is appropriate or inappropriate behavior enters into the experience of the neighborhood or parish. In such a community, people bring hopes and expectations of a style of liturgical music, festival, and the unique attitudes of interpersonal relationships into the assembly at Mass.

For example, for Nicaraguans, it is appropriate to focus on the feast of the Immaculate Conception during the weeks before Christmas. For Mexicanos, it is appropriate to focus on the feast of Our Lady of Guadalupe during the same time. The expectations of celebrating these devotional feasts in an assembly that also practices the European-based season of Advent draw the faithful to consider their cross-cultural reality. The liturgical music director is challenged to choose liturgical music that can express this reality. It is a challenge to celebrate the liturgy with all these in mind yet maintain the simplicity and character of the Roman rite.

To celebrate the liturgy well within a cross-cultural parish, the liturgical music leader needs to learn and teach the music of various cultural groups. It makes sense to prepare a hymn or song written by a Hispanic composer in the style of the composer's musical community and teach it to the parish community at large. One could translate the text; however, translating texts of a hymn into another language is not the full expression of cultural liturgical music. The full expression involves the sounds, harmonic colors, the spirit of the song, as well as the melody and text. That means, in this case, Hispanic musicians who make this music need to teach and lead the music.

What unites Catholics in a cross-cultural parish is the universal Roman Catholic rite—the Mass in which we celebrate the paschal mystery and the mission Christ left to us. We celebrate unity as Catholic people within diversity of sound, language, and people.

99.	*How can the liturgical musician plan a liturgy in which the members of the assembly speak three or four different languages?*

Dealing with cross-cultural elements in the liturgy is more complex in communities with many recent immigrants. The liturgical music director considers the whole picture: the parish at large and the sub-communities that naturally gather because of language and cultural practice. Among a gathered people whose primary language is Spanish, Vietnamese, Tagalog, Korean or Russian, will the English language of these people's new country help them to express their faith and to be formed by it in the liturgy? Does the parish need to celebrate and sing the Mass in their languages when possible to help them express their faith? What about English-speaking children of these recent immigrants?

Alternating languages and music in a dominantly English-speaking liturgy might seem to be a way to celebrate the cultural diversity of everyone. But, a Vietnamese person listening to one reading in English, singing a psalm in Spanish, hearing the other reading in Vietnamese, and praying the eucharistic prayer in English and Tagalog can limit that person's expression of faith. Regular weekly experiences with liturgies in which languages are alternated in this way may weaken the formative power of the liturgy for the people of God who speak only Vietnamese or Spanish.

Some argue that because recent immigrants moved to this country, the liturgy must be in the language of the dominant culture, that is, English. Yet, who would deny the overwhelming response of an assembly when the Mass is celebrated in a person's primary language when possible? Could not the very large parish celebrate its unity in diversity in the parish setting in the same way the universal Catholic church celebrates it throughout the world? Could there not be unity in the Roman rite and diversity in its expression?

The Milwaukee Symposia for Church Composers: A Ten-Year Report talks about three challenges for parishes experiencing cross-culturation. First, the parish needs to develop liturgical music resources that are accessible to all language groups in the parish. That means the parish develops music leaders from among the people, provides hymnals or worship aids, and develops a parish-wide repertoire. Leaders must take care that all these resources are equally shared. Second, the parish needs to encourage the various groups to respect and use each other's music. However, singing each other's music is far from inculturation. The document says this experience "can serve as a bridge" into the language and sounds of beauty of another culture, a "way to enter into their image of church, of salvation, and of the paschal mystery itself" (MSCC 63). Third, the parish needs seek out and to develop multi-lingual music. But, "concern to balance the various languages must be matched by attention to ritual flow and the integrity of liturgical units. Without this, simply alternating languages often results in a melange of unrelated elements instead of a unified liturgy" (MSCC 59).

However, there are parish events, such as the American feast Thanksgiving, in which an attempt to celebrate the multi-cultural identity of the parish could make sense. A music director would be careful not to get into "choir-shifting," in which one language-group choir sings during the presentation of gifts and another during communion. Varied languages may be represented by the different choirs of each language group, but, as always, the choir does not exist to sing to the assembly but to enhance the assembly's song. The assembly could be taught to sing short phrases and to understand the text of another language group, which the music leader would include in the parish repertoire throughout the year.

What about using the melody of one culture and translating the refrain in various languages? One could translate the acclamations of the liturgy, the text of which everyone has memorized, such as the Holy. It seldom works to use one song or hymn in one language in a cross-cultural setting. However, weaving three or four songs (one verse each) into one key to produce one song event can work. Here, the liturgical music leader needs to know music theory well.

The cross-cultural experiences of people in today's California cities, for example, are very different than the cross-cultural experiences of a third-generation Irish-American living among other European-Americans. The presence of Asian cultures—Filipino, Vietnamese, Samoan, Cambodian—in the midst of Mexican, Central American and Spanish-Californian, and African-American families represents a diversity and a challenge as well as a great opportunity for the liturgical musician.

Most of what we deal with as liturgical musicians in the American culture is cross-cultural music.

100. Why should we bother to do music of other cultures?

When a substantial number of Catholics of another culture exist within the parish, it is their right and duty to express their faith in the fullest way possible. It is also the responsibility of parish leaders to enable this expression of faith. It is a simple act of justice to lead a whole parish to embrace change and learn to grow from it. Because justice involves right relationships between human beings as individuals and as communities, the first place we practice it is in the Christian family around the twin tables of word and sacrament.

When we celebrate the liturgy, our hearts, minds, and eyes are opened so that we will recognize and identify justice and injustice when we see it. We practice injustice within the liturgy itself when we ignore the presence of Catholics of another culture or suggest that they belong at an ethnic parish across town. After all, the liturgy is the place where we are constantly changing because we practice becoming Christ for the world. Liturgy and liturgical music must cause continual change in our ways of seeing the world. When we experience that, we are in the process of life-long conversion to see the world with God's sense of justice. The liturgy converts us into the Body of Christ for the world.

101. Can the liturgy and liturgical music really convert people?

Good liturgy has the power to move a person from individualism and possibly isolationism to community. We purposefully do things in our liturgy to convert each person to the idea that no one person is in this world for his or her own sake. We are all meant to see ourselves as part of a much larger entity. Each person is part of a community concerned for the common good of all people.

Liturgy is, after all, action. Active participation in the liturgy is a practice in becoming part of a community of like-minded, spiritual people. A member of a Catholic assembly should be a busy, singing, responding, processing member of an active community. As a result, liturgy cannot be boring. It is interesting, fascinating, absorbing, captivating, engaging. It commissions believers to carry the mission of Christ into the other parts of the world.

We might complain that we don't have "community" in our liturgy, but the reality is that when we celebrate the Catholic liturgy, our celebration is part of a world-wide communal expression of faith that is uniquely Roman Catholic. No Catholic parish is an isolated community because each is part of the universal community—the church.

That is why music for the liturgy cannot be only from one culture or region or of only one or two composers. The liturgical musician today must imagine standing on a spiral time-line where one can see the past, the present, and the future. Envision all the music ever written for the liturgy and ask: Which music will help our assemblies remain connected to the past but still actively participate in the present? Which music will continue to convert people into members of this believing community who will always consider the common good of all? Which music will urge this community of faith to look forward to the future with the kind of hope that continues to build the kingdom of God on earth? Which music will urge members of our community of faith to go into ordinary life and transform it into a community of justice and hope and love which cannot turn away from people who suffer for lack of food, clothing, shelter, healthcare, and education? Working for the common good of all people means that family habits change, that work environments change, that the economy changes, that the priorities on national and international spending changes, that relationships between nations change—that the world changes.

And it can begin in the liturgy we sing.

Even if you are poor, even if you are too poor to buy books,
even if you have books, but have no time to read,
at least remember the psalm refrains that you have sung,
not once, twice, or three times, but so often,
and you will gain great consolation from them.

See what an immense treasure the psalm refrains open to us!...
I exhort you not to leave here with empty hands
but to gather up the refrains as though gathering pearls,
to keep them always with you, to meditate on them,
to sing them all to your friends...

St. John Chrysostom

Annotated Bibliography

Book of Blessings. Collegeville, Minn.: The Liturgical Press, 1989. Another book published by decree of the Second Vatican Council, the *Book of Blessings* contains blessings for the family, a married couple, children, an engaged couple, parents before childbirth, parents of an adopted child, the sick, missionaries, catechists, students and teachers, etc. There are also blessings for buildings, tools, animals, fields and flocks, and at planting time. There are blessings for things in a church and feasts and seasons, and there is a category to catch everything else in the world you might want to bless, "For Various Needs and Occasions."

Chupungco, Anscar J. *Liturgical Inculturation: Sacramental, Religiosity, and Catechesis.* Collegeville, Minn.: The Liturgical Press/Pueblo, 1992. Chupungco, a Benedictine scholar, writes this volume, a sequel to *Liturgies of the Future: The Process and Methods of Inculturation* (1989). In this book, he addresses questions on inculturation, reviewing definitions, the process of inculturation, and methods of inculturation. He talks about sacramentals and popular devotions in the experience of liturgical inculturation. His final chapter deals with inculturation of liturgical catechesis. His Filipino roots aid in his discussion, having experienced the struggle for a truly Filipino expression of the Roman Rite in his native land, influenced by Spanish colonization and post-WW II America.

Constitution on the Sacred Liturgy. In *The Documents of Vatican II*, edited by Walter M. Abbot. New York: Guild Press, 1963. This was the first document of the Second Vatican Council and is the foundation for the restoration of the entire liturgy. Every liturgical musician should read this document over and over again. The most important principle in the document is no. 14, which says that the "Church earnestly desires that all the faithful be led to that full, conscious, and active participation in liturgical celebrations called for by the very nature of the liturgy." It asserts that this is so important that full, conscious, and active participation is to be considered the aim before all else. This is the document that changed the role of the people in liturgy and the nature of music. This is the document that opened the door for Catholics all over the world to celebrate the liturgy in their native tongue for the first time in centuries.

Cotter, Jeanne. *Keyboard Improvisation for the Liturgical Musician, Book One*. Chicago: GIA Publications (74704 S. Mason Ave., Chicago, IL 60638), 1993. Jeanne does an excellent job explaining very basic theory and then guiding the pianist through a step-by-step process toward improvisation on liturgical music. She uses current liturgical music examples of Haas and Haugen and includes some of her own compositions.

Diess, Lucien. *Spirit and Song of the New Liturgy*. Cincinnati, Ohio: World Library Publications, Inc. (2145 Central Parkway, Cincinnati, OH 45214), 1970. The prelude to Deiss' recent book, *Visions of Liturgy and Music for a New Century*, this book was an important tool for the parish musician of the time (and is still helpful reading for some today.) Father Diess describes ways to implement the vision of the Second Vatican Council with music in the liturgy. He talks about the ministerial function of liturgical music, the important role of the singing assembly, the choir director\cantor, and the place of various kinds of music in the liturgy. He discusses acclamations, the responsorial psalm, the processional psalms, litanies, hymns, the creed, and singing the Scripture in liturgy. His final two chapters help musicians make the transition from ways of thinking about instruments for the liturgy and Gregorian chant from the past to the present and future. (The epigraph by St. John Chrysostom is from this book.)

———. *Visions of Liturgy and Music for a New Century*. Collegeville, Minn.: The Liturgical Press, 1996. Diess discusses the ministerial function of music, the role of the assembly and music ministers, and ways of thinking about the use of liturgical music in the parts of the Mass. Father Diess's knowledge of liturgical history and its music enriches the reader as he discusses each aspect of the liturgy. A theologian, liturgist, and composer, he served as a liturgical expert in the Second Vatican Council. His experience with the pre-Vatican II liturgy and his commitment to the process of its restoration impels him to propose well-grounded ideas about the liturgy for the future. His own musical compositions were translated from his native French into the principle languages of the world. This book seems to be an update of his previous book, *Spirit and Song of the New Liturgy*.

Fine, Larry. *The Piano Book: Buying and Owning a New or Used Piano*. 3rd ed. Boston: Brookside Press, 1995. Everything you would ever want to know about pianos is in this book: how the piano works, what to consider before you shop for a new piano, how pianos differ in quality and features. There is a consumer's guide to new and recently made pianos and a guide to buying a used piano. With the information on moving and piano servicing, the reader will indeed know everything one needs to know to purchase a piano for the church.

Grout, Donald Jay, with Claude V. Palisca. *A History of Western Music.* 5th ed. New York: W. W. Norton and Company, Inc., 1996. This book gives the reader an overview of music history and, of interest to the liturgical musician, some historical information on chant, psalm tones, psalms, acclamations, sequences, and early church hymnody. It includes a history of the organization of music and the role of the Catholic Church in the preservation of culture and music. The rest of the book traces the history of music from ancient Greece through Christianity to the twentieth century.

General Instruction of the Roman Missal. In *The Sacramentary.* New York: Catholic Book Publishing Co., 1985. The Second Vatican Council leaders described the way liturgy is supposed to be celebrated in these pages of the sacramentary. There is information regarding the purpose of the gathering song, the kind of bread to use in communion, the order of processions, and much more. Clarifications about music resulting from actual practice were published in later years by the American bishops in *Music in Catholic Worship* and *Liturgical Music Today.* The GIRM should be read by planning teams, presiders, and musicians.

Hughes, Kathleen. *The Monk's Tale: A Biography of Godfrey Diekmann, OSB.* Collegeville, Minn.: Liturgical Press, 1991. For an insight into the Second Vatican Council through a book that reads like a novel, take up this one. Diekmann, a monk of St. John's Abbey in Minnesota, played a distinctive role in the promulgation of the *Constitution on the Sacred Liturgy,* the first document of the Second Vatican Council. Through the biography of this celebrated man, the reader has a glimpse of the church in the years leading up to the Council, of Diekmann's experience confronting a public gathering in Germany where then little-known Adolf Hitler spoke, and of Diekmann's call to fill in after the death of liturgist Virgil Michel, OSB, and to continue as resource and visionary for the restoration of the liturgy. Diekmann's stories about the opening sessions of the Council enlighten the reader about the very human side of the men who faced the vote of centuries which led to the restoration of the liturgy in our time.

Instruction: Inculturation and the Roman Liturgy. Fourth Instruction. Issued by the Congregation for Divine Worship and the Discipline of the Sacraments on March 29, 1994. The purpose of this document is to deal with the principles for adaptation in the liturgy and to outline ways for following through with the directive. The term "adaptation" is changed to "inculturation" for reasons explained in the document. In it we find the directives for inculturation set out with a description of places in the world where inculturation of the liturgy might take place. The hope of the writers is that this description will be considered the only correct procedure for the implementation of inculturation of the liturgy.

Joncas, Jan Michael. *From Sacred Song to Ritual Music: Twentieth-Century Understandings of Roman Catholic Worship Music.* Collegeville, Minn.: The Liturgical Press, 1997. Joncas's well-organized discussion of music documents of the twentieth century is a must for the student of liturgical music. He includes two documents not produced by Rome or the Bishops' Committee on the Liturgy; however, the two reflect recent discussions of American composers and practitioners on recent understandings about worship music. The book offers a perspective on the parish liturgical musician's role in the past thirty to forty years in the church, when shifts in the ways of doing and viewing and living the liturgy at times proved a great challenge to the relationships among leaders in the parish.

Jones, Cheslyn; Geoffrey Wainwright; and Edward Yarnold, eds. *The Study of Liturgy.* New York: Oxford University Press, 1978. This is an excellent source book about the history of the Christian church. It encompasses not only Catholic but Protestant history, in particular the Anglican Church. The book opens with a theology of worship by J. D. Crichton. Following sections discuss the development of these categories from New Testament times to the present: liturgy, initiation, Eucharist, ordination, the divine office, the calendar, and a discussion on music architecture and vestments.

Jungmann, Josef A. *Mass of the Roman Rite.* 2 vols. Westminster, Md.: Christian Classics, Inc. (P.O. Box 30, Westminster, MD 21157), 1986. This is a history book of the Catholic Mass from the time of the earliest church manuscripts up to the 1940s. Jungmann's book was referenced in the work of the Second Vatican Council and is valuable to scholars and practitioners today. A Jesuit professor of Theology at the University of Innsbruck, Jungmann witnessed the Nazi invasion of Austria, which abolished the theological faculty at the university and destroyed the college library. In his humble new residence in Vienna, he began these two volumes in the fall of 1939 in the midst of the Second World War, compiling his previous study, writings, and professorial notes. He completed it in the spring of 1945. It presents the history of the Mass and its theology and ceremony in great detail with extensive footnotes.

Lectionary for Mass: Introduction. Chicago: Liturgy Training Publications, 1998. Every liturgical musician should read these pages. This recently revised and expanded introduction is a detailed description of the Liturgy of the Word with discussions about the three cycles of readings, the liturgical seasons, the way to choose and use psalms between the readings, the alleluia, and the verse before the Gospel.

Levine, Mark. *The Jazz Theory Book.* Petaluma, Calif.: Sher Music Co. (P.O. Box 445, Petaluma, CA 94953), 1995. A pianist can use this book more comfortably than one who doesn't play piano. This is the most comprehensive theory book I've seen. It outlines basic theory, how to practice scales, and how to work with the basic II-V-I progression in music. Beyond these basics is detail on how to improvise at the piano and reharmonize a song.

Liturgical Music Today. Washington, DC: United States Catholic Conference, 1982. Ten years after the publication of *Music in Catholic Worship*, the American bishops published this document reflecting ten more years of pastoral practice celebrating the liturgy of the Second Vatican Council in the United States. In it, they were able to comment on sacramental rites not included in the earlier document, clarify music issues not seen in the previous work, and comment on new issues in liturgical music. This document describes music in the liturgy and guidelines for the use of music and kinds of music in the liturgy of the Second Vatican Council.

The Liturgy Documents: A Parish Resource. 3rd ed. Chicago: Liturgy Training Publications, 1991. A valuable resource for the parish liturgical musician, this book contains the most essential documents written on the liturgy: *Constitution on the Sacred Liturgy*; *General Instruction of the Roman Missal*; *Lectionary for Mass: Introduction*; *General Norms for the Liturgical Year and the Calendar*; *Music in Catholic Worship*; *Liturgical Music Today*; and *Environment and Art in Catholic Worship*. Don't overlook important information in the general introduction of this edition, which helps the reader to distinguish the various natures of the documents. John M. Huels, OSM, clarifies that there are three kinds pertaining to documents of the universal church and two kinds pertaining to the church in America. His discussion helps the reader to prioritize the primacy of one document in relation to the other.

Mahony, Roger. Gather Faithfully Together: A Guide for Sunday Mass. Chicago: Liturgy Training Publications, 1997. Convinced that the liturgy of the Second Vatican Council is not yet fully realized, Cardinal Mahony's pastoral letter paints a clear picture of what parish liturgy should look like. Although written for the leaders of parishes in the Los Angeles archdiocese, this well-written document gives the parish council, liturgy committee, and parish liturgical musicians an opportunity to arrive at a unified vision of the liturgy in the future of the parish.

The Milwaukee Symposia for Church Composers: A Ten-Year Report. Chicago: Liturgy Training Publications (1800 North Hermitage Ave., Chicago, IL 60622-1101), 1992. A gathering of church composers ten years after the publication of the document *Liturgical Music Today* discusses issues that arose in liturgical music between 1982 and 1992. Noting the terms used for music in the liturgy this century, moving from sacred music to liturgical music, which indicated an evolution in ways of perceiving and implementing music in the liturgy, the group proposes the term "Christian ritual music" to indicate an understanding of the structures of the rites and their need for music. The document moves beyond a discussion about which elements to sing in the liturgy to "how we are to sing our rituals." (7) Although the document was not published by the American Catholic bishops, it offers a worthy discussion of the issues related to Christian ritual music and offers challenges to musicians involved in parish ministry.

Musicae Sacrae (Sacred Music). Encyclical of Pope Pius XII on Sacred Music. December 25, 1955. In this document, Pius XII reviews the question of sacred versus profane music, considering the musical forms that developed since the implementation of Gregorian chant into the liturgy. He notes the introduction of the organ and other musical instruments for use during the Mass. Identifying the power of devotional hymns sung in the vernacular of the people, he affirms this practice, which occurred outside the celebration of the Mass, and justifies their use because they serve as a sort of catechism. He affirms that popular hymns sung in the language of the people can be sung after the Latin liturgy had been sung. Besides affirming such deviations in language, he affirmed the presence of women and girls in Catholic choirs.

Music in Catholic Worship. Washington, DC: United States Catholic Conference, 1972, 1983. This was the first of two documents published to clarify ways of using music in the liturgy. It established guidelines for liturgical musicians and pastors for evaluating the selection of music and prioritizing music in the parish repertoire. It clarified and described the ministry of musicians in the liturgy and their relationship to the singing assembly.

Pius X. *Tra le Sollecitudini* (also called *Inter Sollicitudines),* issued *motu proprio et ex certa scientia.* November 22, 1903. This document can be read on-line at www.ewtn.com. Take time to read this document in which Pius X articulates a vision for liturgical music in his future, our present time. Here we find the first use of the phrase, "Filled as We are with a most ardent desire to see the true Christian spirit flourish in every respect and be preserved by all the faithful, We deem it necessary to provide before anything else for the sanctity and dignity of the temple, in which the faithful assemble for no other object than that of acquiring this spirit from its foremost and indispensable font, which is the active participation in the most holy mysteries and in the public and solemn prayer of the Church" (from the introduction).

Rite of Christian Initiation of Adults. Chicago: Liturgy Training Publications, 1988. Catholics have a renewed way of thinking about the celebration of the sacraments of initiation since the publication of these rites. The RCIA highlights the important role the domestic church and the parish church has to evangelize, to renew the faith of Catholics, and to call more Christians to commit to the mission of Christ. One can use the parish repertoire of psalms, hymns, and acclamations in the celebration of the rites.

The Rites of the Catholic Church: As Revised by Decree of the Second Vatican Ecumenical Council. Vol. 1. New York: Pueblo Publishing Co., 1976. After the Second Vatican Council, the rites had to be re-written to "encourage the people of God to understand and participate more fully in these sacred celebrations" (vii). This book was published based on article nos. 14 and 21 of the *Constitution on the Sacred Liturgy.* It contains rites essential to planning liturgical celebrations: Christian initiation (baptism, confirmation, holy communion), penance, marriage, anointing of the sick, rite of funerals, and the institution of readers and acolytes in preparation for priesthood. This is an important resource book for parish liturgy planners and the liturgical musician.

Seid-Martin, Sue. "Singing the Body of Christ." *The Choral Voice* 5, no. 4 (1996): 4. This article is a thoughtful reflection on the focus of all leaders of the liturgy: the singing assembly. Seid-Martin articulates a vision that inspires parish musicians to move beyond concern for the welfare of the music ministry and into a constant concern for the spiritual and musical health and formation of the singing assembly.

Index